Sahajo Bai

SAHAJ PRAKASH:

The Brightness of Simplicity

Sahajo Bai

SAHAJ PRAKASH:

The Brightness of Simplicity

Edited and Translated by
Harry Aveling and Sudha Joshi

MOTILAL BANARSIDASS PUBLISHERS
PRIVATE LIMITED ● DELLHI

First Edition: 2001

ISBN: 81-208-1775-3

Also available at:

MOTILAL BANARSIDASS

41 U.A. Bungalow Road, Jawahar Nagar, Delhi 110 007
8 Mahalaxmi Chamber, Warden Road, Mumbai 400 026
120 Royapettah High Road, Mylapore, Chennai 600 004
236, 9th Main III Block, Jayanagar, Bangalore 560 011
Sanas Plaza, 1302 Baji Rao Road, Pune 411 002
8 Camac Street, Kolkata 700 017
Ashok Rajpath, Patna 800 004
Chowk, Varanasi 221 001

Printed in India

BY JAINENDRA PRAKASH JAIN AT SHRI JAINENDRA PRESS,
A-45 NARAINA, PHASE-I, NEW DELHI 110 028
AND PUBLISHED BY NARENDRA PRAKASH JAIN FOR
MOTILAL BANARSIDASS PUBLISHERS PRIVATE LIMITED,
BUNGALOW ROAD, DELHI 110 007

Contents

Acknowledgments

The starting point for this project was the series of Hindi discourses on the poetry of Sahajo Bai given by Osho Rajneesh in 1974, *Bina ghana parat phuhar* (Rajneesh Foundation, Poona). These have been recently published in English translation as *Showering Without Clouds* (Rebel Publishing House, Poona 1998). Our own translation of Osho's discourses on the poetry of Sahajo's sister-disciple, Daya Bai, *The Last Morning Star*, will appear with the same publisher on Guru Purnima in the year 2000. We would like to record here our gratitude to Swami Yoga Pratap Bharati and Ma Deva Harito for their assistance with this earlier project.

It was Osho's wish that the Hindi poets on whom he spoke should be translated into English. Harry Aveling first decided to study the poetry of Sahajo Bai in 1986 when he was attached to the Department of Religious Studies, the University of Queensland, but the project could not be carried forward because of various practical issues. Dr Richard Barz of the Australian National University provided textual assistance and much encouragement at that time, and has continued to do so over the years. The project finally became a reality when Dr K.G. Verma of Hans Raj College, University of Delhi, kindly took Aveling to the Charandas and Sahajo Bai temples in Hauz Qazi, Old Delhi, on 10 February 1998, making it possible for us to have complete access to the texts of Sahajo Bai and Daya Bai for the first time. The kindness of the guardians of Sahajo Bai's legacy touches us deeply.

The translation was completed collaboratively at La Trobe University, Melbourne, where Mrs Sudha Joshi served as Head of the Department of Hindi until the end of 1999. The Hindi text was prepared by Mr Richard Delacy, under Sudha Joshi's guidance. The Introduction was written at the University of Maryland (College Park), where Aveling served as Visiting Associate Professor of English in Creative Writing during the Fall Semester of 1999. Professor Marian Quartly helped with the computer work involved in preparation of the final manuscript. Dr Aveling is most grateful to Dr Phillip Thomas and Dr Patricia Afable for their gracious hospitality in Chevy Case, Maryland during that time, and to Professors Daniel and Anne Gold for their kindness to him in Ithaca, New York. Both of us wish to thank Ms Carla Taines and Mr Derrick Stone for their editorial, design and technical assistance. The cover photograph was taken by Mr Arjun Tolli, now resident in Melbourne.

Sahajo states at the end of Part 5:

> *Sahaj Prakash* is a small book,
> inspired by the greatness of Charandas.
> Whoever reads or hears it with love
> will never be troubled by sin.

Those named above and many others have made this book a place of peace in a rapidly changing world.

Dr Harry Aveling
Mrs Sudha Joshi MA
23 April 2000

Introduction

This book is intended to introduce the work of the now relatively unknown Hindi devotional poet Sahajo Bai to readers of Indian literature and those interested in Hinduism through the provision of a contemporary translation of her major work *Sahaj Prakash*. The original text is also given for comparative purposes.

Sahajo was a leading disciple of Charandas, one of the great Hindu spiritual masters of eighteenth century Delhi. Her very name suggests "simplicity", "ease", and "naturalness". In accordance with these characteristics, the poetry she wrote is marked by its simplicity of style and its directness of emotional expression. Osho Rajneesh, whose discourses focused new attention on Sahajo Bai's poetry during the 1970s, has described her as "a very ordinary, simple-hearted woman", with no pretensions to literary or philosophical greatness. Rajneesh spoke on her work, however, because he believed that "she was awakened". He commented: "Just her wakening is valuable, everything else is not worth a penny. However great a scholar you may be, if you are sleeping you are of no use. And even if you know nothing but you wake up, then all knowing has happened" (Osho 1998: 70).

It is our hope that this book will enable the work of this devotional woman poet to be better known and appreciated within India and abroad, and that readers will use the book in many different ways, academic and creative, as seems most appropriate to them.

I

Charandas

The major topic of *Sahaj Prakash* is Sahajo Bai's devotion for her guru, Charandas (his full religious name was Ram Charandas, "the servant of the feet of Rama"). The American scholar Daniel Gold, author of a major study to which we are much indebted, *The Lord as Guru: Hindi Sants in North Indian Tradition* (1987), has stated that "Sahajo's guru-devotion is, indeed, legendary". Gold notes that besides "reflecting intellectually on the transformative power of the guru", Sahajo also "treats practical problems of guru-devotion at length: obeying the guru's orders, disobeying them, and grasping 'the guru's word'" (Gold 1987: 82).

Charandas provides a succinct autobiographical sketch of his own life in his work known as the *Jnanaswarodaya*:

My birth was in Dehra
They called me Ranjit.
Muralidhar's son and
A Dhusar by caste.
To Delhi I came
As a child.
Roaming about I met Shukdev
Who called me Charandas.

(Gold 1987: 67, from Dixit 1966: 130)

Ranjit Singh was born in 1703 CE at Dehra, near Alwar in Rajasthan. His caste status is ambiguous. Although he acknowledged membership of the "Dhusar" merchant caste, he has often been referred to as a "Bhargava" as well. This caste claims descent from Bhrigu, the Vedic seer. Ranjit could also have been considered, therefore, as an "ambivalently pure" Brahmin (Gold 1987: 68).

When the boy was about five years old, his father is said to have died. Muralidhar apparently had the habit of going off into the forest to meditate. As Gold simply notes: "one day he never came back" (1987: 68). The father may have suffered an accident. Alternatively, he may have impetuously decided to join up with a group of wandering ascetics. There is, of course, no way we can tell. In either case, as a consequence, Ranjit's mother, Kunjo Rani, moved to Delhi to join her parents who had recently settled there. Charandas spent the greater part of the rest of his life in Delhi, when he was not touring. His mother presumably lived in the precincts of his temple too and is praised several times in Sahajo's poetry.

Despite Muralidhar's early disappearance, the influence of his example was decisive for his son. As a teenager, Ranjit himself for several years often went outside the city where he lived, to meditate and seek initiation to the ascetic life. At nineteen, Ranjit became a disciple of the individual Sahajo describes in the first poem in this volume as "grandfather Shukdeva ji". In Poem 83 (these numbers have been added to the text for ease of reference), she spells out the full lineage of disciplic succession to which she claimed allegiance:

Great grandfather Videha was the supreme teacher.
Shukdev initiated my Master.
Sahajo's prostrations to you, Charandas, my guru,
accept my homage.

The names of the lineage have potentially multiple references. Videha may have been a human renunciant but the name is also the name of the Vedic king who is sometimes called Janaka. Sahajo describes him in Poem 80 as the founder of Sankhya philosophy. Shukdeva may well have been an ordinary mendicant. W. Crooke (1896: 202) refers to "Baba Sukhdeva Das, a faqir of high religious attainments", who initiated Charandas at Shukra Tal near Muzaffarnagar. Drawing on the *Swarodaya*, and incidently casting an interesting light on one aspect of Charandas's name, G.A. Grierson (1910: 366) describes how:

> the saint took the lame youth on his shoulders and after carrying him some distance, initiated him as a disciple, teaching him the Rama-mantra, or initiatory formula of the Rama worshippers and instructed him in faith in God (*Hari-bhakti*) and knowledge of the Supreme (*Brahma-jnana*).

The description of the initiation marks it as being "the traditional Hindu style of a proper Vaishnava initiation" (Gold 1987: 72).

Charandas himself believed that Shukdev was far more than a mere human sadhu. He identified his preceptor with the divine Shukdeva, the perpetually youthful son of Vyasa, who had divided the *Vedas*, recited the *Mahabharata* and composed the *Upanishads*. Capable of manifesting himself at different times in history, Shukdev had appeared to the child Ranjit while he was still in Dehra, and then in his adolescence pointed him to Shukra Tal, the place of his future initiation, and the same place where Shukdev had originally explained the *Mahabahrata* to King Pariksit (Gold 1987: 72). There was a further sociological and religious significance to this conjunction of master and disciple. As Gold (1987: 69) explains: "For Charandas to affirm Shukdev the son of Vyasa to be his guru ... is to affirm his links as a Bhargava to the Mahabharata and ultimately to the Veda. In Shukdev, Charandas finds a direct link to the origins of the Hindu tradition through an appealing and unsullied source". (The psychological links of an abandoned son finding a spiritual father in the wilderness where his own father had disappeared are also worth some consideration.)

Following this initiation, Charandas practised various forms of yoga for fourteen years, including Patanjali's eight-limbed yoga, raja yoga, bhakti yoga and sankhya yoga. Gold (1987: 72) describes this as "a long period of non-Vaishnava ascesis". However, the nature of his initiation, and the reference to the regular practice of bhakti yoga, throw some doubt onto this assertion. It should especially be noted that these practices accord very closely with the statement by Krishna in the *Shrimad Bhagavatam* that there are "only three ways of liberation laid down by me ... knowledge, yoga and devotion" (A.C. Bhaktivedanta 1976: 122). This threefold combination occurs frequently in Sahajo's poetry as her summary of his teachings and practice. It would, therefore, be a fitting reward for his devotion to Hari that, some time in middle life, while visiting the holy land of Vraj Charandas was granted a vision of the Lord Krishna, as well as a further revelation of Shukdev. These visions were considered by his biographers to be major events in his life (Gold 1987: 71 and 227 fn. 42).

While firmly grounded in traditional brahmanic scriptural studies, Charandas taught a popular mixture of ritual Hinduism mixed with the radical openness of the iconoclastic, individualist sant poets. He was also a prolific writer. The principal collection of his writings, *Bhaktisagar*, begins with an interpretative description of the land of Vraj, and includes Hindi adaptations of five upanishads, the story of Nachiketa from the *Brahmanda Purana*, extensive descriptions of hatha yoga practices, as well as verses in the sant style, and so on (Gold 1987: 69).

In the middle of the nineteenth century, H.H. Wilson (1861: 178–9) described the tenets of "the Charandas sect" at some length:

> Their doctrines of universal emanation are much the same as those of the Vedanta school, although they correspond with the Vaishnava sects in maintaining the great source of all things, or Brahma, to be Krishna: reverence of the guru, and assertion of the pre-eminence of faith above every other distinction, are also common to them with the other Vaishnava sects from whom, possibly, they only differ in requiring no particular qualification of caste, order, nor even of sex, for their teachers ...

After a digression, Wilson then continued: "Another peculiarity is the importance they attach to morality, and they do not acknowledge faith to be independent of works ..." Finally, having discussed the Charandasi moral code, Wilson concluded:

> The other obligations enjoined are, to discharge the duties of the profession or caste to which a person belongs, to associate with pious men, to put implicit faith in the spiritual preceptor, and to adore Hari as the original and indefinable cause of all, and, who, through the operation of Maya, created the universe, and has appeared in it occasionally in a mortal form, and particularly as Krishna at Brindavan.

These teachings, together with Charandas' own personal charisma and opulent monastic life-style, tended to create an image of him as a centre of Hindu orthodoxy at a time when the forces of Islam weighed heavily upon the citizens of Delhi and the northern plains. Beside his religious achievements, Charandas is often praised for the firm stand he took against the Mughal emperor and the invasion of the Persian Nadir Shah (Gold 1987: 74). In Sahajo's confident words (Raga 23):

> The True Master holds high status in the world,
> even kings and emperors bow before him.

Sahajo Bai

Just as Shukdev had done to him, Charandas "whispered the mantra" (Raga 2) to the young woman whose poetry was to sing his fame. As a result, "He [Charandas] made me 'Sahajo'", as Poem 83 states, or, as we further spell out the ambiguity in our translation, "He established me in simplicity". If Sahajo had another name before she took to the ascetic life, we never hear of it.

The name "Sahajo" occurs regularly as a signature to various poems throughout the *Sahaj Prakash*, and is commonly used when she comments on some matter she has just discussed ("Sahajo says ..."). Now and then, as we have just seen, the senses of "simplicity", "ease" and "naturalness" also make a perfectly good alternative in the reading of certain poems. Sometimes (where the metre requires it) she calls herself "Sahajo Bai", to the same end of commenting on the matter in hand. Often the diminutive form of address, "Sahajiya", Little Sahajo, appears as a way of noting something, often something complex, which Charandas has said to her. Conversely, on the cover of the 1979 edition of *Sahaj Prakash*, she is reverently referred to by her traditional title, "Shri Shukdev Sampradaya Acharya Hari Bhakta Sahajo Bai Ji", Teacher of the Shri Shukdev Lineage and Devotee of Hari, the venerable Sahajo Bai.

Her family connection to Charandas has been much discussed. In Poem 84, she describes herself only as "Hari Prasad's daughter" and, like Charandas, "born in a Dhusar family". She may have been Charandas' first cousin, the daughter of his father's sister (Gold 1987: 81, citing Ganga Das' introduction to *Sahaj Prakash* 1979). It seems unlikely that she was his sister, "as is said by some", which Grierson (1910: 366) notes but rejects. Bose (1986: 153) not only describes Sahajo as Charandas' sister but, on the "evidence" of their names, accuses them of a "Sahajiya connection". This seems an unjustified slur, if any type of sexual relationship is thereby implied, and Bose presents no other evidence to support his circumstantial claim.

Sahajo was born on the fifth day of the moonlight fortnight of the month of Shravan (July–August) in 1782 VS (1725 CE). She was thus some twenty-two years younger than Charandas. The story is told that her marriage was arranged when she was about eleven or twelve years of age. Charandas was invited to bless the couple and he arrived while she was being dressed in fine clothing and jewellery. No doubt Charandas Maharaj made a striking figure. We can imagine the impression this close but holy relative might have made upon the young girl. He would still have been in his early thirties; perhaps radiant with devotion, physically strong through his practice of hatha yoga, strikingly dressed in orange, and possibly riding on a horse himself, surrounded by his retainers. At any rate, he laughed and said as he looked at her:

> Oh Sahajo, why beautify your face
> For mere married bliss?
> One must die, you cannot stay
> We must all go,
> Of that you can be sure.
>
> (Gold 1987: 81, citing Ganga Das 1979: xiii)

Sahajo immediately replied firmly in response to him that she would not marry but, instead, would live thereafter as a devotee of the Lord. As the bridegroom's party approached, the groom's horse was startled by a fire-cracker, tripped over a branch and fell. The groom died at once. Impressed by what he considered to be Charandas' omniscience, Hari Prasad gave his blessing to his daughter and himself renounced the world, as did his four sons.

In Delhi, the young woman's life was passed in the service of her teacher. She devoted herself to the spiritual practices she mentions throughout the *Sahaj Prakash*. She participated in regular worship and chanted the "*Soham*" mantra at dawn, throughout the day and at the middle of the night. She practised hatha yoga, together with the associated breath-control techniques of pranayama and the use of the inner physiological locks (*bandha*), meditating on "the inner sound" and the various chakras. She listened to readings of the *Shrimad Bhagavatam* on Hari's love for His devotees. In Poem 4 she praises the scripture because it seemed to:

> ... (shine) like the sun,
> when one reads it, or hears it,
> the chains of darkness fall away

Quotations from the *Bhagavad Gitá* occasionally appear in her verse. These readings would have often been done by Charandas himself. There would, of course, have been the regular flow of consecrated sadhus to the temple, and the frequent gatherings of Charandas' initiated followers for the chanting of bhajans. She would have seen the comings too of the less committed, drawn from within and beyond the great capital, with all their joys and sorrows, as well as their myriad of personal mannerisms.

There was also time for the celebration of various seasonal rituals, particularly those honouring Charandas and his mother. Celebrations were held to mark the coming of spring as well. During the revels of Holi, Charandas would prepare the drinks mixed with herbal drugs which were part of the day's inversion of the normally staid patterns of life (and may have formed part of his ascetic practices from time to time). Sahajo even mentions watching various plays on religious themes (Raga 30). In Raga 29, we have a glimpse of her responding with amusement to some words by Charandas on "the name of the guru as the best medicine", and we can imagine that this was a common enough situation:

> Sahajo Bai is happy,
> when Charandas talks like this.

Overall it was, no doubt, a strict life but she never seems to have felt it as harsh. Indeed, at various points in *Sahaj Prakash* she speaks out against more conventional pious behaviour, such as long pilgrimages, the public giving of large donations, worshipping "idols of stone and rivers of water" (Poem 83), the futile intellectual study of "the Vedas, Puranas, and six Shastras" (Poem 28), and twisting the body this way and that in penance (Poem 73). All of these meant nothing to her, she insisted (Poems 16–19), compared to serving the guru and devotion to Hari. These other practices are futile, she says in Poem 73.

If anything, it was probably a rather exciting life-style which this determined young woman from the provinces had chosen for herself. We should not forget, either, that as a young wife-to-be of a husband who had died, life in her home village would have held little joy for her.

There was probably one thing she did not do. In all likelihood, it would have seemed improper for Sahajo to accompany Charandas when he went on his travels. An interesting story is told about one time when Charandas was away on a tour to nearby Shahjahanpur. Sahajo had apparently previously decided that she would not eat her own meals until he had first eaten. As she had no way of knowing now when she should eat, Sahajo became distraught after a few days. Charandas had compassion on her and came to her while she was sitting for her evening meditation. As Gold (1987: 82) tells the story, their conversation went as follows:

'You have come far, Maharaj,' she said, 'and you must be hungry.
Let me bring you some food.'
'But it's the middle of the night,' answered Charandas. 'How can
you have anything ready?'
'There are some sweetmeats downstairs.'
'All right. Go get them.'

After eating a few, he offered some to Sahajo, who gratefully accepted them, not having eaten at all during his absence. He then gave her his bracelet and told her to call everyone in the house to have his darshan. When they arrived, however, Charandas had vanished.

Whether they did come or not, when it was clear that Charandas was absent, the story says that people laughed at her and called her crazy. It may be suspected that this was perhaps not an unusual reaction to her behaviour. We find her writing, for example, in Poem 76:

The world called Sahajo mad
people began to leave her ...
Men and women laughed at Sahajo
but her mind was filled with bliss.

At the same time, this rejection was also a frequent experience in the poetry of Mira Bai. To give only one example:

They thought me mad for the Maddening One,
raw for my dear dark love,
coloured with the colour of my Lord ...

(Hawley and Juergensmeyer 1988: 134)

The presence of a strong-minded young woman in the temple of a rich and powerful ascetic would surely of itself have set tongues wagging.

At any rate, the bracelet remained, even if Charandas did not. It later became known that Charandas had said that same night in Shahjahanpur that Sahajo was so devoted to him she should have his bracelet (Gold 1987: 82–3).

By the time of his death in 1782 CE, Charandas had a following that spread to the Punjab and far into the Gangetic plain. The organisation of the main temple and its material holdings passed to a leading disciple, Juktanand, who was both a scholar and a man of proven administrative ability. Siddha Ram, a disciple of Ramrupji, another of Charandas' senior disciples, filed a suit against Juktanand in the court of Shah Nizamuddin, disputing the legitimacy of Juktanand's claim to succeed Charandas. After a month's deliberation, the judge resolved that the temple would go neither to Juktanand nor to Ramrupji, but to Sahajo Bai. She would have been almost sixty years old by this time.

For a short time, the decision seemed satisfactory. But then Juktanand's followers attempted to gain control of the temple once again. On hearing of this, Siddha Ram came running, armed with a staff. Sahajo filed a complaint against both parties and the temple was closed for a short time. Eventually she was allowed to return to the temple and to live there again. She was, however, only permitted to use a side gate, as the main gate was closed to all. This compromise, too, pleased no one. Finally the judge decreed that Sahajo should live in a separate house, as Juktanand and Ramrupji already did (Gold 1987: 83–4). The house in which Sahajo Bai passed her last days still stands in Charandas Marg, Hauz Qazi, Old Delhi.

II

Sahaj Prakash

As we have already seen, Charandas was a prolific poet in the popular language of Delhi, and used his poetry to teach a wide range of religious truths. Sahajo was not alone among his disciples in following her master in this artistic practice. Ramrupji was the author of a doctrinal work entitled *Guru Bhakti Prakash*. Another senior disciple, Jogjit, also wrote a biography of Charandas, *Shri Lila Sagar*, although this was a "longer and more anecdotal work" (Gold 1987: 67). Sahajo's sister-disciple, Daya Bai, wrote a small volume of verses, together with a long poem of 105 verses praising various bhakta devotees, *Daya Bai ki Bani* (Gold 1987: 67, 86).

Charandas' literary advice to Sahajo seems to have been simple and straightforward:

> Sahajo,
> reveal in your songs those things which
> when read or when heard
> will help human beings
> escape their afflictions.
>
> (Poem 44)

Following the plan suggested by the Hindi text, the translation here has been divided into seven parts. The first five parts constitute the original version of *Sahaj Prakash*. The eighty-five poems are written in the simple verse forms known as *doha* (couplets) and *chaupai* (quatrains).

Part 1 consists of poems praising the Guru and describing various forms of the Guru–disciple relationship. Part 2 deals in graphic terms with human suffering, for the purpose of encouraging her listeners to adopt the classical moral virtue of detachment from the world (*vairagya*). Part 3 is concerned with spiritual heroism (*satya vairagya*) and describes a range of spiritual practices which can strengthen those resolved to turn their back on the endless human suffering described in Part 2. The brief Part 4 deals with theological matters drawn from Sankhya philosophy, describing the divine in terms of the abstract concept of *satchidananda*, knowledge, truth and bliss. These doctrinal topics are continued in Part 5, where Sahajo encourages readers to move from philosophical contemplation to the practice of devotion. This movement from intellectual doctrinal matters to daily practical devotion parallels the similar shift between Parts 2 and 3 earlier.

The last poem in Part 5 announces the completion of the *Sahaj Prakash* on the eighth day of the first lunar fortnight of the month of Phalgun (February–March), 1800VS (1743 CE). Remarkably, Sahajo would have been only eighteen years of age at this time, and would have spent only six or seven years with Charandas to this point in her life.

The two further parts to the volume were presumably written later in Sahajo Bai's life. Part 6 presents two sequences of *kundaliya* stanzas, longer verses which include the repetition of the second half of the second line at the beginning of the third line. These poems are loosely based on series of days and numbers, and Sahajo associates them with various moral and religious teachings. The first series deals with sixteen facets of the light half of the lunar month (including the new moon and the full moon). The second deals with the seven days of the week. They touch on themes found in the earlier parts of *Sahaj Prakash*: the briefness of human existence and the necessity to submit oneself to the guru.

Finally, Part 7 is a collection of almost forty *ragas*, written for various times of the day and seasons, as well as for the various festivals such as Holi and Charandas' birthday. Because of their greater complexity and sophistication it seems likely that these ragas were written throughout Sahajo's adult years, while the poems on days and numbers may have come perhaps fairly soon after the major part of the volume.

On the whole, Sahajo's poetry is indeed simple and direct. She has a youthful confidence in her own ideas and experience, which are often profound, although at other times shaped by a rather literal religious imagination (which Charandas himself seems to have possessed) and a predictably limited knowledge of life. Her poetry is strongly physical. In particular, it is extremely visual. "Seeing truly" and "not seeing at all" are major themes which run throughout the volume. In Poem 83, towards the end of Part 5, Sahajo, exclaims:

> The true guru gave me eyes. It is certain.
> I know because I have seen it for myself.

This is an important reminder of the importance of "seeing" the sacred, literally and with the eyes of the soul, which is present throughout the whole of the Hindu religious tradition (Eck 1998).

This desire to see truly interconnects her focus on the role of a guru in human life, with her graphic presentation of the consequences of the other choices which people make in their daily activities. Although Part 2 may strike some readers as extremely pessimistic, and therefore too long, Sahajo's attitude to her teacher is undoubtedly moving and, after a strong beginning in Part 1, finds its fullness in the mature ragas of Part 7. In a subtle way she also struggles in the last part of the book with her feelings, as a woman, towards the man for whom she gave up everything and lived near, in a condition that was commonly misunderstood by the society around her. This pathos intensifies the significant degree of spiritual insight shown at various points throughout the whole of the book, which arise from her genuine commitment to the religious and literary disciplines of the paths of yoga and bhakti devotion.

The Basic Assumptions of *Sahaj Prakash*

The basic assumptions of the volume can now be sketched in more detail. The world we see and experience is one of interminable birth, suffering, death, punishment and rebirth. This process is driven by the relentless power of karma, arising from the mistaken identification of true reality with the ego which is created by the senses and the mind. True reality consists of the underlying immortal and unchanging spirit, which exists within and beyond every person, but cannot be seen with the physical eyes. Rather, the gift of recognition is granted to those who recognise their own spiritual nature through the grace of the true guru, the satguru. These fortunate few are freed from the necessity of enduring endless birth and rebirth. They pass their days in the practice of the spiritual disciplines (*sadhana*) of "knowledge, yoga and devotion". They are the saints (sants, or sadhu using the term in its broadest sense), and they live most blissfully when they have each other's company, centred around their commitment to the guru, enjoying the good company of satsang, praising the Lord and hearing stories of His pastimes.

Let us now briefly examine each of these themes as Sahajo uses them in her poetry.

THE BODY

The human body provides "a rare opportunity" for finding God by bringing one's desires to rest in the guru (Poem 73). If one can do this, one can live in the stage described in "the Vedas and Puranas" (especially the *Mandukya Upanishad*) as the "fourth", fully awakened, beyond sleep, dream and deep sleep (Poem 43). Poem 80 states:

> Awake, asleep and dreaming,
> these are the three stages of life.
> Together they shape the body,
> as it decreases, increases and decays.
> The soul should look beyond these
> to the fourth stage
> which the mind and senses cannot understand.
> Sahajo says:
> its nature is limitless.

In Poem 78, Sahajo insists that the lives of most people are lived out in an unconscious, mechanical way:

> Those whose souls have not awakened
> are people of sleep and dreams.

It is, she explains, the nature of the dream to forget the real world and instead create an alternative world for oneself, "heaven, the mortal realm and hell". These three realms are "built of lies". In them, the ignorant seek to enjoy themselves, but they are perpetually caught up in the pains caused by change and illusion. In a series of striking images, Sahajo compares the world to a "mirage", in which the ignorant childishly believe they are drowning; then to "a heap of rubies,/ drawn on paper"; and, finally:

> The world is like
>   an army of stars
>   in the dawn sky.
> Sahajo says:
>   they will not stay.
> Like a pearl made of dew,
> like water in the hollow of your hands.
> The mind makes a fortress of smoke
> and creates a glorious kingdom there.
> It is a game of hide and seek, Sahajiya,
> nothing happens. No truth is told.

At the centre of the illusion is the sense of embodiment, of giving priority and credence to the flesh and its experiences. Sahajo's view of the body is cyclical and pessimistic. "We are born eighty-four lakh times", she states, "and each time we die" (Poem 43). Each birth offers us only "great pain/ and many sorts of terror" (Poem 43).

In itself, the rare and "precious jewel of a human birth" (Part 6, Day Fourteen) is only one possible type of birth. Using "old numbers/ set a long time ago", Sahajo lists the total number of births which each soul must endure as including "nine hundred thousand water creatures", "ten lakh creatures which fly", "eleven lakh worms and insects", "twenty lakh immovable creatures", "thirty lakh animal births", and finally "forty lakh human births" (Poem 72). Literally a "lakh" is 100,000. In general usage it is simply a very, very big number. Sahajo's figures (120 lakh, in fact) already far exceed "eighty-four lakh", the number she constantly uses in her verse to count the cycle of birth and rebirth. Moreover, "eighty-four lakh" is not the end of the matter. Those who fail to find liberation are condemned to "endure/ another eighty-four lakh births" (Poem 43).

Sahajo's description of the nature of human existence, as found in Part 2, is extremely glum.

The human body is at the mercy of the senses, which are constantly tempted by the sensual vices to which Sahajo frequently points: "desire, anger, attachment, greed and pride". These vices intoxicate the mind and shape the ego (poem 53). Identification with the body is further reinforced by one's social roles, which change throughout life, and by "the web of the family" (Poem 30) which also provides an ongoing constellation of different roles and insistent obligations.

The unborn child lives in the cramped, uncomfortable and undignified environment of the mother's womb, "between excrement and urine" (Poem 45). The child suffers one disease after another (49). When he (and the poems seem more oriented to masculine experience, although had Sahajo chosen to describe female experience the poems may well have been even more pessimistic) is five, he is sent to school, where he is constantly beaten and humiliated by the teacher (51). The youth is carried away by his own desires and wastes his time in sensuality, passion and arrogant self-assertion, foolishly boasting of his intelligence, physical strength and prosperity (52–53). Marriage brings the burden of maintaining a family, the desire for honour and respect for one's achievements, and the humiliating experience of never having enough money and therefore always being dependent on others for the smallest of favours (54). The web of relationships which begins when the child is bound to his kinsfolk (47) is intensified now that the man has his own family and relatives to care for (55).

Finally, old age brings physical decay (56), and rejection by those whom he has loved and for whom he has worked so hard (57). Only death remains. Just as one cannot stop others dying – "If she was yours,/ why did she die?", Sahajo demands in Poem 41, "Why couldn't you protect her/ forever?" – neither can one avoid dying oneself.

At the time of death, Yama comes with his clubs. He drags the soul away to judgement and the "fifty-six forms of punishment" (64). Those who die before their appointed time is fulfilled, because of an accident, disease, famine, suicide or murder, will be condemned to wander as ghosts until their proper time finally arrives (65). Sahajo's description of the life of ghosts is similar to beliefs still held in North India. Having died in great pain, ghosts are characterised by their eagerness to inflict pain on others, as well as their love of unclean, polluting places, such as cemeteries and burial grounds (R. and S. Freed 1993: 80).

The world is false, "a web/ woven with lies" (Poem 41), Sahajo insists. Somehow people live in a continual state of expectation that all their dreams will be fulfilled, all their hopes realised. Using a familiar agricultural metaphor, several poems also compare human desire to the growing of grain. In Poem 41 Sahajo points to the farmer who hopes "for a rich crop" as long as "there is rice in the husk", without realising that the world is simply "an empty husk". The crop that "animals and birds,/ humans, gods and demons,/ movable creatures,/ immovable creatures,/ insects and grasshoppers" do, in fact, produce is karma, which is the result of our inclinations and desires. Our inclinations work against the development of good karma. In Poem 74, Sahajo states:

When the deer of attachment
lives in the body,
no crop can grow in the field.
As soon as the seeds are sown,
they are gone.

Finally one's karma also determines one's rebirth in the next world. Humorously she warns those who want to be reborn in a temple that they may become a rat and live in a house, those who want to be surrounded by fair women that they may be reincarnated as a dog in a household of lepers, and so on (Poem 42). Few remember Ram throughout their life and are able to call on him at the time of death. They will thus be unable to live devout lives in the company of the saints when they are reborn, let alone aspire to "meet with Hari" and never be reborn at all, never die (Poem 43).

THE SPIRIT

It is the world which we see with the eyes of the spirit which truly matters. The identification with the body is wrong:

> ... the wise know a secret:
> the body is false,
> only the soul is true.
>
> (Raga 21)

The body consists of many parts, being divided from "head to toe, and it dies". The soul is immortal, "it pervades the body/ and is indivisible" (Poem 41). Behind the endlessly disappointing and continually frustrating appearance of life and death lies another existence, which is formless and eternal, the realm of the spirit.

Sahajo calls this divine life by many names, including "Parabrahma", "Brahma", "Satchidananda", "Purusha and Prakriti", "Ishwara", "Hari", "Ram" and "Krishna".

The Vedantic titles do not appear very often in Sahajo's poetry. Brahma is "the formless one", who is "indivisible". He (or "It") "pervades the body" and is "beyond all that we can think" (Raga 18). Everything "is Brahma" (Poem 81). The person who renounces the pleasures of the world and meditates on God-without-Form "knows Brahma" (Poem 39) and sees "with Brahma's eyes" (Poem 80). The one who worships the guru "becomes Brahma in an instant" (Raga 1).

The term "Brahma" sometimes refers to the Supreme Spirit but also sometimes to the god with four faces. The Poem for the Tenth Day of the Lunar Cycle points to a different mythological discourse about Brahma the Creator, when it notes that the world is like "a bubble in the ocean":

> Like the egg of Brahma
> in the vastness of Brahma's body.
> Like the egg of Brahma in the vastness of Brahma's body
> with no limits, this side or that.

In common with all other living creatures, it is also Brahma's destiny to die one day (Poem 73). Some of the poems also refer to Brahma's four sons.[1]

---

1 We have followed Sahajo in the translations when she blends the Vedantic abstract Brahman with the deity named Brahma. On the other hand, when Sahajo discusses death, in Poem 64 for example, she separates Yama from Dharmaraj; we have kept this too. Our aim has been to represent Sahajo's religious aesthetic, not "correct" it.

Part 4 considers "Satchidananda" in the terms of negative theology. Sahajo struggles in Poems 79 and 80 to describe the Supreme in terms of confusing paradoxes. In Poem 79 she states that: It is "never new, never old", not subject to death, indivisible, autonomous, "it needs no one,/ it rules no one", it has no caste, no form, no colour, no body, no creed, no home", and so on. Towards the end of the poem she writes:

It is Brahma, without a beginning,
    O, Sahajiya,
To reach its depths
    is a terrible task.

It performs no rites,
    it wears none of the six philosophies.
It has no qualities, no defects,
    O Sahajiya,
Purusha, Supreme Spirit, is indescribable.

It has no form, no name, no qualities,
It has nothing to do with the five elements.

The use of the affectionate name "Sahajiya" should make us realise that this is Charandas speaking, Sahajo is not speaking on her own behalf. Indeed she adds:

My guru Charandas has seen all this,
Sahajo sees nothing, may God forgive her.

But her confusion is not hers alone. It is the confusion that even the gods share when they try to understand Hari. In Raga 32 (where the four-faced deity is certainly limited in what he knows), she states:

No one understands the mystery of Hari

Shiva, Brahma, and all the gods,
    tried to solve this riddle –
He is "not that", "not this",
    say the Vedas.
Brahma came again as a child,
    and exhausted himself in asceticism.
Shiva practised Yoga and meditated intently,
    without success.

Shesha, Saraswati, Indra and Ganapati
worshipped Him,
without understanding who He is.
Kamadeva, Narada, Sanaka and the other sons of Brahma,
adorned themselves with devotion.
The wise, the moral, rishis and munis,
Shiva, sidhas and sadhus,
Said Charandas,
the pandits bearing their books
are like donkeys, Sahajo Bai.

The theme of the intellectual inaccessability of spirit even to the gods, who are presented in somewhat comic terms seeking to find what they can never find, also appears in ragas 37 and 38.

This does not mean, however, that the Supreme is indifferent to human existence or inaccessible to those who see with ordinary eyes. Poem 79, on Satchidananda, ends with the injunction, not to study, but to "drown yourself in the passionate love of the Lord", a theme explored in some detail in Part 5. In this part of the work, she rejoices that Ishwara has manifest itself by taking on recognisable human forms. God-without-Form has become God-with-Form through playing "many parts" and adopting many "guises", especially the "complete incarnations" of Rama and Krishna:

For the sake of his devotees,
Hari comes
to free the earth of its burden.
He protected the good,
he killed the evil.

From God-beyond-Form
He became God-with-Form
to deliver the saints.

(Poem 81)

This is, of course, the teaching of *Bhagavad Gita* 8: 4: "To deliver the pious and to annihilate the miscreants, as well as to re-establish the principles of religion, I advent Myself millenium after millenium" (translation of A.C. Bhaktivedanta 1976: 69).

In sant usage, Ram[2] is a common term for God-without-Form. Ram

2 Our translation uses this familiar daily pronunciation, without the final "a" sound – except where that is useful for the metre.

is the "Lord of liberation" (Poem 37). He is also the true Creator. In using the name of Ram, Sahajo is not referring, or only tangentially referring, to the hero of the epic *Ramayana*. Her only extended portrayal of Ram does not show him as a warrior, the husband of Sita and brother of Lakshman, but in the gentler role of one who created the world, and the body, to be gardens and who cares for them (The Seven Days of the Week, Tuesday).

As the true Creator, he is the one whom mankind forgets through the false constructions of his dreams and wakening fantasies. Poem 41 warns:

> If you abandon Ram,
> and create your own world
> Sahajo says,
> You will lose everything.

Raga 28, too, has the chorus: "Wicked man, having abandoned Ram, you created the world".

The name Sahajo most uses for the divine is "Hari". This occurs as a synonym even in poems where the names Brahma and Ram are also mentioned. Poem 81 states:

> everything is Brahma.
> Hari revealed.
> Hari concealed.

Raga 24, which uses the chorus, "only the name of Ram can save me", moves easily to the praise of "Hari's Name" as "the essence of the Vedas", "supreme in the three worlds", insisting that it "destroys sins, purifies the heart,/ cleanses the mind, it can make you mighty". The names are alternatives to each other, rather than the names of separate divine beings, different gods.

The specific name of Hari appears in four distinct contexts. First, "He is the source of all there is" (Raga 10), the Creator. Second, he is the subject of many stories, which are dear to the sants because of their power to transform the devotee (see especially Poem 40). "Keep good company", she suggests elsewhere (in the kundaliya poem for Monday), "and hear stories of Hari,/ Hear stories of Hari, nothing else matters". Sahajo does not, in fact, mention what these stories are, although the reference early in *Sahaj Prakash* to *Shrimad Bhagavatam* makes it perfectly clear which stories she has in mind.

Third, it is the name of Hari which the sants constantly chant. Raga 2 candidly declares:

I know nothing of other religions.
    I simply chant "Hari ... Hari".

The description of "Commitment to the Truth" in Part 3 centres on the details of how one should chant: continually, silently, and with awareness. Among the injunctions of Poem 73 are:

Sahajo says:
    when you chant the name of Hari
    keep Him hidden in your heart.
Lip should not touch lip,
no one should know.

Poem 77 provides quite a technical description of how the mantra can be moved around the chakras so that "the unchanted gayatri" constantly pervades the body, creating endless ecstasy. In chanting, the meditator is filled with light, like the sky covered with brightness even when there is no lightning, or a gleaming pearl shaped without a shell (The Phases of the Moon, Six). For the saints, it is Hari's name chanted at the time of death which releases the enlightened soul into a peaceful transition, safe from Yama's violent ways (Poem 41).

Fourth, the name of Hari is the intimate distinguishing mark of the guru and his work in his community. Raga 8 describes the purpose of the true guru as to "establish Hari-bhakti". Hari, in fact, "dwells in the guru's house" and without the guru, one cannot find Hari (Poem 28). The guru is so powerful that he can "force Hari" to come to the longing devotee "at once" (Poem 27). Under the guru's influence, the bodies of the saints exist in the world, but their minds "have the form of Hari" (Poem 34).

THE GURU

It is the manifestation of the personal, loving human form of God as the Guru which most captures Sahajo's heart. Nowhere, as has been repeatedly stressed, did Sahajo find love more manifest than in her guru. The praise given to Charandas and Shukdev throughout the volume is overwhelming. Her prayer to "grandfather guru Shukdev ji" to reveal "the ultimate mystery" to her (Poem 1), includes an immediate reference to Charandas through mention of the guru's feet (*charan*) in the opening line. The guru is "the true form of Brahma". He is "unfathomable, impenetrable". He is the Lord of the three worlds and reveals the inner world of those who come to him. He guides seekers to the other shore of the terrible ocean of birth and rebirth. He is beyond the three gunas. He bestows knowledge, devotion and wisdom. Whoever takes refuge in him, "dwells in the beyond,/ Lives in wisdom" (Poem 2).

Sahajo's treatment of "the practical problems of guru-devotion" (Gold 1987: 82) in Part 1 leads her to expound on such topics as types of gurus, types of the human intellect, the good disciple, the undeserving disciple, those who blaspheme the guru, and the wicked. Her presentations rest on the moral dichotomy of the good and the saved, set against the wicked and those doomed to suffering. Even Sahajo's images are practical.

The four types of guru, for example, are the "touchstone" guru, "Malaya mountain" guru, "lamp" guru" and the "bhringi" guru. The touchstone guru can turn base metal into gold. The Malaya mountain turns trees growing near it into sandalwood. The lamp guru can enlighten the disciple with the touch of his inner flame. The bhringi wasp wraps itself around its victims and, by laying its eggs inside them, turns them into itself (Poems 5 to 7). The human intellect is like a trickle of water, endlessly rushing forwards and disappearing; a path, which is soon erased by passing vehicles; a row of stones, which will naturally decrease but never add to themselves; or a drop of oil, spreading across water.

The good disciple is like clay in the hands of a potter, or a toy, which moves as its owner directs (Poem 29). The good guru is impartial like a washerman, a rain cloud, or a block of ink (Poem 30). One must accept his very command and follow him completely (Poem 15). On the other hand, no matter what the guru does for him or her, the undeserving disciple will not change but will remain clay, dead wood, unlit, untransformed (Poem 31). Those who slander the guru are like ghosts, who wander about in broad daylight, erasing the traditions, failing to understand the scriptures, and turning their back on dharma. Even if they are called sadhus, they are wicked, filled with pride and self-righteousness, arrogant about their own learning, and dismissive of the glory of devotion to Ram (Poems 23 and 24).

Nowhere is Sahajo's devotion to the guru more striking, more paradoxical, more determined, or more wonderful, than in Poem 11:

> I might leave Rama, I could never forget my Guru.
> In my eyes, Hari is not the equal of my Master.
> Hari brought me into this world,
> the Guru freed me from the cycle of birth and death.
>
> Hari sent five thieves with me,
> the Guru released me from their power.

Hari entangled me in the web of my family,
the Guru broke the chains of attachment.

Hari bound me with disease and the love of life,
the Guru made me a yogi and freed me from this.
Hari confused with karma and dharma,
the Guru showed me my own soul.

Hari hid himself from me,
the Guru gave me a lamp and showed me God.
Above all, Hari created bondage and freedom from bondage,
but the Guru freed me from all these illusions.

I offer my body and mind to Charandas,
I will never leave my Guru, I might leave Hari.

In itself, the paradox is not new. In one of the well-known poems of Kabir both God and the guru appear before the disciple. Confused by the problem of whom he should bow down to first, the disciple finally bows before the guru, because it is the guru who has shown him God. Sahajo's poem is gentler, more playful, perhaps more feminine. It is, as Rajneesh (1998: 41–42) remarks, "a loving reproach", spoken with "great love", a subtle quarrel between "two lovers" which has nothing to do with logic. "Just think", Osho asks, "how can she put him lower? Can one who cannot put her master lower than God put God himself lower than the master? Impossible!"

Charandas and Krishna

The name "Krishna" appears only in two poems in the core *Sahaj Prakash* text. In Poems 81 and 82, Sahajo is concerned to describe "the role of bhakti in removing doubts about God-with-Form and God-beyond-Form", as the heading explains. (This limited focus on Krishna in Parts 1 to 5 may also suggest that the revelation of Krishna to Charandas at Vraj only occurred towards the end of the time of the writing of the *Sahaj Prakash*, or even later.)

Throughout most of Poem 81, Krishna is the philosopher of the *Bhagavad Gita*, the source of all life, indivisible, all pervasive, unchanging, accessible to those who seek him through yoga or wisdom. Sahajo, however, again lovingly insists:

"The yogi finds me through yoga.
The wise finds me through the mind".

Sahajo says:
I found Him through devotion.
I found Him through love.

The Krishna she has found is not the philosopher but the cowherd child raised by Yashoda and Nanda, who danced with "the cowherd girls" and "played games with the cowherd boys" (Poem 82), the adorable child of the tenth canto of the *Shrimad Bhagavatam*.

In a striking development, the ragas seem to blur the persons of Charandas, Hari and Krishna without any discrimination, just as the earlier poems blur references to Hari, Brahma and Rama. In Raga 5 she describes Charandas as "Hari ... disguised as a man". When she celebrates Charandas' birth in Raga 7, he is a particular "soul ... come in the form of a man", manifest in the Dhusar line, "Gopal, dressed in the body of a sadhu", come in order to "to return the world to the path of true religion".[3] In Raga 8, Sahajo describes Charandas as the incarnate true guru, "the avatar", come to establish "Hari-bhakti in Kaliyuga".

A much more complex process in which the adorable child Krishna is physically identified with the true master Charandas unfolds in some other ragas in Part 7.

Let us begin with Raga 9. Here we have a detailed description of "Natavara dancing,/ Madan, the thief of hearts." Sahajo first mentions his crown, quickly passes to "his large ear-rings/ briefly glimpsed through his curls", the pearl at his nose, before talking of the movement of his lips and eyebrows. The shift from the things which Krishna wears to what he does leads into the centre of the raga, through the following references to the "quickness of his feet", the skill with which he raises his arms, and the sound of his ankle-bells, "tata-thei, tata-thei". "He was enchanted", Sahajo insists, "and he enchanted us all".

What she writes next is, however, completely unexpected:

Charandas lives in Sahajo's heart.
Make me your home, Shuk Muni Rai,
  Lord of Delight and Restraint.

We might want to read this as saying that not Krishna but Charandas lives Sahajo's heart, although it would be hard to justify this distinction in terms of the works we have just quoted. The underlying logic would rather seem to be that Charandas is the same Krishna whom she finds so enchanting.

---

3 Compare this with the end of *Bhagavad Gita* 8: 4 cited above.

The identification of Krishna with Charandas is also clear in Raga 15. In this lyric, Sahajo describes the bliss of an ecstatic experience received in meditation. The references to "the place where the three rivers meet" (the place where the psychic channels of the ida, pingala and sushumna nadis join), and drinking "the nectar stream" (the bliss of deep meditation), place the poem in the area of the yogic imagery which has been explored in the earlier parts of *Sahaj Prakash*. But there are two further moves which complete the text, neither of which is purely yogic.

The first is the consequent vision:

> A radiant child was there, resplendent like a god.
> invisible, incomprehensible, and I worshipped him.

The child might be Hari, given Sahajo's delight in the child Krishna. But the second move is completely unexpected. The poem concludes:

> I bowed and gazed on him for a very long time.
> Guru Charandas raised his hand.
> and I was content.

The child is Charandas. The Krishna whom Sahajo adores is both the playful child of Vrindavan and her teacher in Delhi.

Loving the Divine

Another American scholar of Hindi literature, John Stratton Hawley (1986), has argued that, although both male and female bhakti poets attempt to relate to Krishna, the way in which female poets write is significantly different from that used by male devotees. Mira's discourse, for example, employs "a distinctly female type of speech", which is sometimes close to the women's folk songs of her region, and allows for the expression, positive and negative, of a range of experiences typical of women's family life (1986: 237). The distance between Mira's own experience and that of the gopis is not a significant "jump of the imagination". Mira, as a woman, is "already close to the intimacy and natural-ness of spirit that it is the purpose of bhakti (loving devotion) to cultivate" (1986: 238). In so doing, Mira "insists on institutionalizing her defiance of convention by claiming a conjugal bond with Krishna that will challenge and degrade the earthly marriage that she scorns" (1986: 247–8). However, Mira, unlike Sur, often also closely identifies herself with the social roles of the yogi, perhaps because love-struck young girls naturally manifest the state ascetics seek so hard to cultivate:

"sleeplessness, fixity of gaze, inattention to dress, tangled locks, and a great store of inner heat" (1986: 243). She therefore forged yoga and marriage into a new paradoxical institution which would challenge the conventional "anti-structures" of masculine ascetic thought (1986: 250).

Sahajo is continually conscious of her womanhood. As we have seen, she does use a type of speech based on every day reality and family experience which is concrete, vivid and thoroughly physical. It has room for complaint (and even cursing, as in Raga 31 for example) in a manner which is seldom an acknowledged part of masculine speech. This consciousness places her as "a woman without any greatness". Socially, she locates herself as a servant, whose place is by the door, ready to answer her master's call. She begs for a glance. Without him, she has nowhere else to go (Raga 25).

Her attitude to Krishna, however, is very different from Mira's. She does not identify with Radha. Nor does she identify with the mass of the cowherd girls, who were Krishna's childhood friends. Having never had children of her own, or ever apparently wanting to, she cannot play the role of mother (which, in fact, she also projects onto Charandas in Raga 26.)

Hers is a chaste contemplation of the divine presence, undertaken from a distance, true *darshan*. Her relationship with Charandas, even if he were Krishna, was shielded, she believed, by the celibate nature of her religious calling. Raga 36 states:

> I have only Śhri Gopal,
> I see no one else.
> He lives in my heart,
> I care for no other.
> Everything I have is his,
> is his, is his, is his.
> I have abandoned the modesty of my caste,
> I am not worried what others may think.
> I was a bride, between two families,
> and no one could stop me.
> Love lives in my body,
> I am his disciple,
> The bonds of love protect me
> they will never break ...

Yet this lyric too has another surprise ending, which is made possible not by Krishna bhakti but by the apparently irrefutable logic of Vedantic non-duality. If everything in the universe is One (Poem 39), if "Hari's people" live "without attachment/ in non-duality" (Poem 40), if God-with-Form and God-beyond-Form "are not two, are not different" (Poem 82), if "the worship of the self" was the best worship and "there is none greater" (Raga 16), then surely it was possible also to argue that there was no ultimate distinction between herself and Charandas. Boldly, Raga 36 concludes:

> I am become Charandas[4]
>   I have no thoughts or actions of my own.
> Sahajo no longer exists.
>   The two are one,
>   there is no duality.

The same insistent claim appears in the beautiful Raga 38: "There is no Sahajo Bai, there is no Charandas", because "there is no duality". These are claims of non-physical, spiritual intimacy. Perhaps Charandas accepted them graciously, perhaps he found them embarrassing. We cannot say.

The extent of the emotion concealed in this illogical logical Vedantic claim breaks out with great force in Poem 76, entitled "The Beginning of the Description of Aspects of Love", and in Ragas 14 and 15, which are similar to the earlier long poem. Their apparent subject is the experience of drinking "the cup of love", the Holi narcotics, mixed by Charandas' own hand. The undertaking leaves her blissful, but also totally deranged and carried far beyond her battered body. There is a passionate quality to these works which should not be dismissed too quickly or judged too readily.

Hawley (1986: 250) has suggested that if the world called Mira crazy, she returned as good as she got and that "the world had it coming". The same might be said, to an extent, of Sahajo Bai. Living in the temple as a celibate woman, she too challenged the common view of the value of earthly life, of the domestic role of women in the world, and of the relationship between humanity and God. If she played dangerous games, in which she felt that "the feet fall here, the feet fall there", completely beyond her control, she was, at the same time, also confident that "Hari always takes care of them" (Poem 76).

---

4 "I have become Charandas" is more grammatical in English, but our translation attempts to capture an ongoing identification which is beyond time past.

III

The Method of Translation

There are many different ways of translating literary texts.

There is the very literal. It is possible to translate an original text closely, almost word by word, although more difficult, of course, to bring the rhyme and metre of the original into English. Ludmila Rosenstein's study of *The Devotional Poetry of Svāmī Haridās* (1997) provides closely literal translations. An example of Rosenstein's method of translation, and a very clear sample of the type of the erotic masculine writing Sahajo was so strenuously avoiding, is the following (Rosenstein 1997: 300):

> Her breasts are jugs, her youth is blossom, the spring is kept covered by her bodice and garment.
>
> A palace of qualities, she is sitting in a garden of beauty, her face shining,
>
> Bihari has the loveliness of myriads of cupids; by seeing him all suffering is destroyed.
>
> Such a connoisseur is Haridas' sovereign; she came to embrace him and they united, smiling.

While the translation is no doubt accurate (although the "cupids" are rather strange), it scarcely excites the reader as poetry. To be sure, it is scarcely intended to do so.

Other translators have sought to be both poetical and literal, by retaining the foreignness of a poem from a distant time and cultural setting in a deliberately archaising poetic style of the receiving language. This is what Baldoon Dhingra does in his translation of one of the ecstatic lyrics of Mira (1977: 60), with its dignified style, inversions of grammar, archaic "thees" and "ohs", and the panoply of Victorian poetry and hymn writing:

> In life, no less than in death,
> Thou art my friend.
> I shall never depart from Thee
> For I am lost without the vision
> Of Thy Effulgent Presence.
> Ask my heart, it will tell Thee
> That I climb higher and higher
> Always seeking a glimpse of Thee,
> I have spent many a night weeping,
> Oh, what is this world but a false

Elusive thing, a shadow play.
Family, friends, all are false.
I stand before Thee, then,
With folded hands, like a supplicant,
Hear me, listen, oh, listen to my words.
That mad elephant the mind
Breaking loose, roamed at large,
Till the Lord brought it under control.
And now I live continually in His Presence,
Meera's Lord is Girdhar Gopal,
At whose lotus feet she dwells.

Still other writers have made an effort to have their translations of poetry read as contemporary poetry. The late, great translator of Indian literature, A.K. Ramanujan, has argued for a more open, free verse style of translation that is similar to much of the practice of today's poetry in English. In the "Translator's Note" (1967: 11) to his ground-breaking book *The Interior Landscape of the Heart: Love Poems from a Classical Tamil Anthology*, Ramanujan insisted that: "The originals would not speak freely through the translations to present day readers if the renderings were not in modern English, and if they were not poems themselves in some sense."

Ramanujan deliberately chose to translate, not line by line, but rather "phrase by phrase as each phrase articulates the whole". He described his own practice as follows:

> I have paid special attention to the images and their placement. Sometimes I have made explicit typographic approximations to what I thought was the inner form of the poem; broken up lines and arranged them in little blocks and paragraphs, or arranged them stepwise; I have tried to suggest by the spacing the distance or the closeness of elements in the original syntax.

An example of this approach, chosen fairly much at random from the rich harvest Ramanujan offers, is this (1967: 72):

What She Said

Before I laughed with him
    nightly,

    the slow waves beating
    on his wide shores
    and the palmyra

bringing forth heron-like flowers
near the waters,

my eyes were like the lotus
my arms had the grace of the bamboo
my forehead was mistaken for the moon

But now

The original Tamil does not use capitals, punctuation, a narrow grammar or complex end rhymes, and Ramanujan has not felt the need to do so either. Despite their power, Ramanujan's translations deliberately give no sense of the prosodic features of their originals or of their original forms. Ramanujan insisted: "I had to choose between transplanting the physical look of Tamil lines and transposing their patterned internal syntax, and I have invariably chosen the latter course" (1967: 12).[5]

The method of translation employed here follows most closely that of Ramanujan. The translations are very much a collaborative effort. Sudha Joshi prepared literal versions of each poem, and we then went over them together, letter by letter, word by word, line by line. I prepared the poetic renderings in the free verse style presented here, and we discussed (and changed) those together too. In accordance with John Bierhorst's more precise rendering of Ramanujan's practice, we have based the line breaks upon "reiterative features uncovered by precise analysis of the discourse" (1992: 58–9). It should be clear from most of our verses where the limits of Sahajo's two and four line verses rest, how her lines are consistently divided in the middle, and where their rhetorical and personal significance is marked at other points.

The main text we have used is the 1979 reprint of the *Sahaj Prakash*, published by the Shri Shyamcharandas Prakashan Karyalaya, Delhi. We have revised our final text in the light of the 1913 edition, published by The Belvedere Press in Allahabad, held by the Library of Congress in Washington D.C.

---

5 The danger of this approach, of course, is that it is possible to so completely assimilate the source poem to the conventions of modern verse that, for example, Mira may sound, apart from an occasional reference to Govinda or Giridhara, exactly like any other young American writer at their worst, "unrhymed, unmetered, and unshaped" (Dana Gioia 1999: 21).

Conclusion

Sahajo's simplicity, it may be increasingly clear, is not really so simple. Throughout this book, we have felt it important to translate and describe her work as precisely as possible in the present literary context, without imposing other assumptions upon it. Perhaps we should give the last word to Osho, as the original instigator of this project:

> When the content is rich, what you want to say is a diamond, there is no need for it to be embellished with anything else. A Kohinoor can stand alone, it is enough. What else is there to add? If you add anything, its beauty will diminish. Sahajo's words are like the Kohinoor. Their beauty is unparalleled, but it is the beauty of simplicity. So if you try to understand it intellectually then it will not be understood because the mind enjoys complications, it enjoys solving riddles. If you see through your heart, then in this simplicity you will find such mysteries which can never be solved. Enter into it, drown in it – you will be lost. But the moment will never come when you will be able to say that you have known. (Osho 1998: 129)

No translations ever please all readers. We hope that some of these will please some of our readers.

Harry Aveling
Nashotah House
4 October 1999

References and Other Works for Further Study

English Works

A.C. Bhaktivedanta Swami Prabhupada (1968; repr. 1976) *Bhagavad-Gita As It Is*, Abridged edition, Bhaktivedanta Book Trust, New York.

John Bierhorst (1992) "Incorporating the Native Voice", in *On the Translation of Native American Texts*, ed. B. Swann, Smithsonian Institution Press, Washington D.C.

Manindra Mohan Bose (1986) *The Post-Sahajiya Cult of Bengal*, Gian Publishing House, Delhi.

W. Crooke (1896; repr. 1974) *The Tribes and Castes of North Western India*, Cosmo Publications, Delhi.

Baldoon Dhingra (1977) *Songs of Meera: Lyrics in Ecstasy*, Orient Paperbacks, Delhi.

Diana L. Eck (1998) *Darsan: Seeing the Divine Image in India*, 3rd edn, Columbia University Press, New York.

R. Freed and S. Freed (1993) *Ghosts and Castes of North Western India, Life and Death in North India*, Anthropological Papers of the American Museum of Natural History, No. 72, New York.

Dana Gioia (1999) "Notes on the New Formalism", in *New Expansive Poetry*, ed. R.S. Gwynn, Story Line Press, Ashland Oregon.

Daniel Gold (1987) *The Lord as Guru: Hindi* Sants *in North Indian Tradition*, Oxford University Press, New York.

G.A. Grierson (1910) "Charandasis", in *Encyclopaedia of Religion and Ethics*, Vol. III, ed. J. Hasting, T.T. Clark, Edinburgh.

John Stratton Hawley (1986) "Images of Gender in the Poetry of Krishna", in *On the Complexity of Symbols*, eds Caroline Walker Bynum, Steven Harrell and Paula Richman, Beacon Press, Boston.

Osho Rajneesh (1993) "Showering Without Clouds", *Osho Times International*, Vol. 6, No. 21, 1 Nov., pp. 17–19.

Osho Rajneesh (1998) *Showering Without Clouds*, Rebel Publishing House, Poona.

Osho Rajneesh (2000) *The Last Morning Star: Songs of Daya Bai*, trans. Harry Aveling and Sudha Joshi, Rebel Publishing House, Poona.

A.K. Ramanujan (1967) *The Interior Landscape: Love Poems from a Classical Tamil Anthology*, Peter Owen, London.

Ludmila L. Rosenstein (1997) *The Devotional Poetry of Svami Haridas: A Study of Early Braj Bhasa Verse*, Egbert Forsten, Gronigen.

H.H. Wilson (1861: repr. 1976) *Essays and Lectures on the Religions of the Hindus*, Vol. 1, Asian Publication Services, New Delhi.

Hindi Works

Charandas (repr. 1966) *Bhaktisagar*, ed. T.N. Dixit, Navalkishore Press, Lucknow.

Daya Bai (repr. 1967) *Daya Bai ki Bani*, Belvedere Press, Allahabad.

Jogjit (1762; repr. 1968) *Shri Lila Sagar*, Shri Shukcharandasiya Sahitya Prakashak Trust, Jaipur.

Bhagwan Shree Rajneesh (1975) *Bina Ghana Parat Phuhar*, Rajneesh Foundation, Poona.

Ramrupji (no date) *Guru Bhakti Prakash*, Virakt Vaishnav Rupmadhuri Sharan, Jugalghat, Vrindavan.

Ramrupji (repr. 1972) *Mukti Marg*, Shri Shukcharandasiya Prakashak Trust, Jaipur.

Sahajo Bai (repr. 1913) *Sahaj Prakash*, Belevedere Steam Printing Works, Allahabad.

Sahajo Bai (repr. 1979) *Sahaj Prakash*, Shri Shyamcharandas Prakashan Karyalaya, Delhi.

सहज प्रकाश

संत शिरोमणि श्री शुकदेव
संप्रदायाचार्या

सु० श्री सहजो बाई जी कृत

1 ॥वंदना॥

कर जोरू परनाम करि, धरू चरन पर शीस,
दादा गुरु शुकदेव जी, पूरन बिस्वा बीस।
परम हंस तारन तरन, गुरु देवन गुरु देव,
अनभै वाणी दीजिये, सहजो पावे भेव॥

2 ॥गुरु वंदना॥

नमो नमो गुरु देवन देवा,
नमो नमो गुरु अगम अभेवा।
नमो नमो त्रिभुवन के स्वामी,
नमो नमो गुरु अंतर्यामी॥

नमो नमो गुरु पातक हर्ता,
नमो नमो पारायण कर्ता।
गति मति छाके आनंद रूपा,
नमो नमो गुरु ब्रह्म स्वरूपा॥

PART 1: THE GURU

1 *Prayer*

With folded hands I bow,
    placing my head at his feet,
grandfather guru Shukdeva ji,
    in whom I rest my trust.
Paramahamsa, supreme ascetic,
deliver me
    from the ocean of birth and death.
Guru of the gods,
    the god of gurus,
Grant me courage,
    give me the words,
Help Sahajo find
the ultimate mystery.

2 *A Prayer to the Guru*

I bow to the Guru,
    god of gods,
I bow to the Guru,
    unfathomable, impenetrable,
I bow to the Guru,
    Lord of the three worlds,
I bow to the Guru,
    he who searches the inner realms.

I bow to the Guru,
    he who destroys all my sins,
I bow to the Guru,
    he who helps me to the other shore,
He whose mind and deeds
    are filled with true bliss,
I bow to the Guru,
    the true form of Brahma.

नमो नमो मम प्राण पियारे,
नमो नमो तिरगुण से न्यारे।
भक्ति योग ज्ञान के दाता,
सहजो के पुरवो सब काजा॥

जो कोई शरण तुम्हारी आयो,
तुरिया तत विज्ञान बसायो॥

3 ॥दोहा॥

निर्मल आनन्द देत हो, ब्रह्म रूप कर देत।
जीव रूप की आपदा, व्याधा सब हर लेत॥

4 ॥चौपाई॥

नमो नमो शुकदेव गुसांई,
परगट करी भक्ति जग माहीं।
श्रीमद्भगवत भानु प्रकाशा,
पढ़ सुन कटैं तिमिर के फांसा॥

ज्ञान योग की 'नौका' कीनी,
चरणदास केवट को दीनी।
बहुतक पापी जीव चढ़ाए,
भव सागर से पार लगाए॥

I bow to him,
        who is dearer than my own life,
I bow to him,
        who is beyond the three gunas.
He who bestows devotion,
        yoga and knowledge,
Please help Sahajo finish
        all that she must do.

Whoever takes refuge in you
        dwells in the beyond,
Lives in wisdom.

3

You give us pure bliss
and bring us to Brahma's form,
when you steal our suffering
and all the afflictions
which living souls endure.

4

I bow to Shukdeva Goswami,
who has manifested devotion to the world.
Shrimad Bhagvatam shines like the sun,
when one reads it, hears it,
the chains of darkness fall away.

You made a boat from the yoga of knowledge
and gave it to Charandas, the boatman.
He took many sinners aboard
and ferried them across the ocean of birth and death.

किरपा वली हाथ में राखें,
काहू से दुर्वचन न भाषें।
अमृत वचन बोल बैठावें,
नर नारी लों पतित तिरावें॥

कलियुग में सतयुग विस्तारा,
रामभक्ति का खोल दुवारा।
सुन २ के जिज्ञाषु आवें,
उनके सब संदेह मिटावें॥

5 ॥लक्षण॥

॥दोहा॥
गुरु हैं चार प्रकार के, अपने अपने अंग।
गुरु पारस दीपक गुरु, मलयागिरि गुरु भृंग॥

6 ॥दोहा॥

चरणदास समरथ गुरु, सर्व अंग तिन माहि।
जैसे को तैसा मिले, रीता छोड़े नाहिं॥

Holding the oar of kindness in his hands,
he never speaks harshly to any man.
He sits with his passengers,
sharing words soaked in the nectar of immortality,
and ferries sinful men and women
across to the other shore.

He has brought satayuga into kaliyugá,
by opening the door of devotion to Rama.
Having heard of his glory, the curious enquirers came,
and he erased all their doubts.

5 *Marks of the Guru*

There are four kinds of guru,
each has his own qualities:
the touchstone,
the lamp,
Malaya mountain,
bhringi wasp,
Guru.

6

Charandas is a powerful guru,
complete in every way.
He gives each person
exactly what they seek
and never leaves anyone
empty.

7 ॥चौपाई॥

लोहे कू पारस हो लागे,
कंचन करें बेर नहिं ताके।
सिष पलास चंदन करि डारें,
मलिया गिरि हो कारज सारें॥

कीट समान शिष्य जो आवे,
भृंगी गुरु निज रूप बनावे।
करें भिरंगी ढील न कोई,
पलटैं रूप "पाछलो" सोई॥

बिना लोय दीपक सिष पर सै,
हो दीपक तिनहूं कूं दरसै।
बकसें अपनी ज्योति उजारा,
होय चांदना भवन मंझारा॥

चरण दास गुरु समरथ ऐसे,
सहजो वाई भाषत जैसे।
सबं गति सब अंग हैं उन माहीं,
उन से भेद छिप्यो कोई नाहीं॥

7

As soon as the touchstone guru
touches iron,
it turns to gold.
As soon as the Malaya mountain guru
touches the *shisham* and *dhak* trees,
they turn completely
to sandalwood.

When the disciple
comes like an insect,
the bhringi guru
turns him
into his teacher's form.

When the guru
who is a lamp
burning without a flame
sees the disciple
and reaches out brightly
towards him,
light shines
in the middle of the house.

Charandas is powerful
in all these ways.
Sahajo Bai tells it truly.
He is complete,
lacking nothing,
and no secret can be hidden from him.

8 ॥दोहा॥

ज्ञान भक्ति, अरु योग का, घट लेवैं पहिचान।
जैसी जाकी बुद्धि है, वैसा देवे ज्ञान॥

9 ॥चार प्रकार की बुद्धि॥

॥चौपाई॥

आप सबन में सबसे न्यारे,
चार बुद्धि के मनुष उचारे।
प्रथम बुद्धि जललोक खिचाई,
खिंचती जाय सोई मिट जाई॥

दूजी बुद्धि लीक रस्ते की,
चलै मनोरथ मिटे हिये की।
तीजी बुध-पाहन की रेखा,
घटै सही पर बढ़ै न नेका॥

चौथी तेल बूंद जल माहीं,
फैलत फैलत फैलत जाई।
छोटी से दीरघ परकासै,
वरन वरन के रंग निकासै॥

तीन बुद्धि जग में दरसावै,
चौथी बुद्धि कोई बिरला पावै।
सहजो बुद्धि सब थोथी कहिए,
हरि गुरु किरपा सब में चहिए॥

8

Knowledge, devotion and yoga,
Whatever you want, he will give you.
When the mind is right,
He will fill you with the wisdom
which most suits you.

9 *The Four Types of Intellect*

He who is superior to all
declared that there are four types of human intellect.
The first is like a trickle of water,
endlessly advancing, leaving nothing behind.

The second is like a well-worn path,
which is soon erased by passing desires.
The third is like a row of stones,
they may wear away, but will never increase.

The fourth is like a drop of oil
which spreads, spreads and spreads in water,
even a tiny speck will shine for a long time,
and sparkle with a myriad of bright colours.

In this world, the first three are common,
the fourth type is rarely found.
Sahajo says that all are hollow,
all need the grace of Hari and the guru.

10 ॥गुरु कृपा वर्णन॥

॥दोहा॥

हरि किरपा जो होय तो, नाहिं होय तो नाहिं।
पै गुरु किरपा दया बिन, सकल बुद्धि नसि जाहिं॥

11 ॥चौपाई॥

राम तजूं पै गुरु न विसारूं,
गुरु के सम हरि को न निहारूं।
हरि ने जन्म दिया जग माहीं,
गुरु ने आवागमन छुड़ाई॥

हरि ने पांच चोर दिये साथा,
गुरु ने लई छुड़ाय अनाथा।
हरि ने कुटुंब जाल में गेरी,
गुरु ने काटी ममता बेड़ी॥

हरि ने रोग भोग उरझायो,
गुरु योगी कर सबै छुड़ायो।
हरि ने कर्म भर्म भरमायो,
गुरु ने आतम रूप लखायो॥

हरि ने मोसूं आप छिपायो,
गुरु दीपक दे ताहि दिखायो।
फिर हरि बंध मुक्ति गत लाए,
गुरु ने सब ही भर्म मिटाए॥

चरणदास तन मन वारूं,
गुरु न तजूं हरि कू तज डारूं।

10 *On the Grace of the Guru*

If Hari blesses you,
    you are blessed indeed.
If he does not,
    you are not.
Without the grace
    of the guru's compassion,
your intellect is wasted.

11

I might leave Rama, I could never forget my Guru.
In my eyes, Hari is not the equal of my Master.
Hari brought me into this world,
the Guru freed me from the cycle of birth and death.

Hari sent five thieves with me,
the Guru released me from their power.
Hari entangled me in the web of my family,
the Guru broke the chains of attachment.

Hari bound me with disease and the love of life,
the Guru made me a yogi and freed me from this.
Hari confused me with karma and dharma,
the Guru showed me my own soul.

Hari hid himself from me,
the Guru gave me a lamp and showed me God.
Above all, Hari created the bondage of sweet maya,
but the Guru removed me from all these illusions.

I offer my body and mind to Charandas,
I will never leave my Guru, I might leave Hari.

12 ॥दोहा॥

सब पर्वत स्याही करूं, घोलूं समंद मझाय।
धरती का कागज करूँ, गुरु स्तुति न समाय॥

13 ॥चौपाई॥

गुरु की स्तुति कहां लों कीजे,
बदला कहा गुरुन को दीजे।
गुरु का बदला दिया न जाई,
मन में उपजत है सकुचाई॥

इन नैनन जिन राम दिखाए,
बन्धन कोटि काट मुकलाए।
अभय दान दीनन को दीने,
देखत आप सरीखे कीने॥

12

If I could make
    all the mountains
    into one block of ink
If I could dissolve them
    into all the oceans
If I could make
    the whole world
    into one sheet of paper
It still wouldn't be enough
    to contain
    my guru's praises.

13

How can I praise the guru enough?
What can I give him
    for all he has given me?
I can never repay his kindness.
When I think of him
    my mind draws back.

When he reveals Ram to these eyes,
    he breaks countless bonds
    and brings me freedom.
He gives the gift of courage to the frightened,
and makes them like himself.

गुरु की किरपा अपरंपारी,
गुण गावत मम रसना हारी।
शेष सहसमुख निसदिन गावे,
गुरु स्तुति का अंत न पावे॥

मौन गहूं स्तुति का करूं,
बार बार चरणन सिर धरूं।
चरन दास महिमा अधिकाई,
सर्बस बारै सहजोबाई॥

14 ॥दोहा॥

गुरु मग द्रढ़ पग राखिए, डिगमिग डिगमिग छांड़।
सहजो टेक टरे नहीं, सूर सती ज्यों मांड॥

There is no end to his mercy.
It would tire my tongue
        to sing all his virtues.
Even if the thousand-headed snake Shesha
        sang his praises
        day and night,
it could never finish singing his glory.

I live in silence,
        what praise can I offer him,
except
        to place my head
        at his feet
        again and
        again?
His glory is so great
that I sacrifice everything to him.

14

Place your feet firmly
        on the path of the guru,
Give up
        your higgledy-piggledy
        ways.

Sahajo says:
        your staff should not falter.
Walk
        like a widow
        into her husband's fire.

15 ॥चौपाई॥

गुरु के प्रेम पंथ सिर दीजे,
आगा पीछा कबहु न कीजे।
गुरु के पंथ होय सो होई,
मारग आन चलो मत कोई॥

गुरु के पंथ पैज का पूरा,
गुरु के पंथ चले सो सूरा।
गुरु के पंथ चले बल योधा,
गुरु के पंथ चलै का बोदा॥

गुरु के पंथ मुक्ति उजयारा,
गुरु के पंथ नहीं संसारा।
गुरु के पंथ मिटै दुख जोई,
गुरु पंथ महा सुख होई॥

चरणदास को पंथ दुहेला,
सनमुख चाले ताहि सुहेला।
गुरू के पंथ चले सत वादी,
सहजो पावे भेद अनादि॥

15

Bow down
    to the path of the guru's love,
Never hesitate.
The guru's path
    is as it is.
You must not follow any other.
Only those who give themselves completely
    can follow the guru's path,
Only the brave
    can follow the guru's path.
Only the warrior
    can follow the guru's path.
No coward can ever
    follow the guru's path.

The light of liberation shines
    on the guru's path.
The worldly cannot walk
    on the guru's path.
Sorrows vanish
    on the guru's path.
Happiness comes to those
    on the guru's path.
The path of Charandas
    is difficult,
But those who walk on it
    never stumble.
Those who tell the truth
    follow the guru's path.
Sahajo says: they find
    the secret
    which has no beginning
    and no end.

16 ॥गुरु चर्णों की महिमा॥

अढ़सठ तीरथ गुरु चरण, परवी होत अखंड।
सहजो ऐसो धाम ना, सकल अंड ब्रह्मंड॥

सब तीरथ गुरु के चरण, नित ही पर्वी होय।
सहजो चरणोदक लिए, पाप रहत नहिं कोय॥

17 ॥चौपाई॥

सब तीरथ गुरु चरणां लारे,
चर्णा मृत ढिंग सदा हमारे।
चरण कंवलकीनिसदिन पूजा,
परसूं और देव ना दूजा॥

इष्ट हमारे गुरु के चरना,
गुरु चरण के ध्यान हिये धरना।
गुरु के चरण लगे सो तारे,
गुरु के चरण प्राण से प्यारे॥

16 *The Glory of the Guru's Feet*

The sixty-eight places of pilgrimage
are found at the guru's feet.
Endless festivals
are celebrated there.

Sahajo says:
there is no other place like them
in the whole
of Brahma's egg.

All places of pilgrimage
are found at the guru's feet.
Every day
festivals are celebrated there.

Sahajo says:
when you drink the water
in which his feet have been washed,
your sins will vanish forever.

17

Pool after pool,
all pilgrimage places
reside at the guru's feet.
The nectar of his feet
is with us always.
I will praise his lotus-feet
day and night
and never submit
to another god.
The guru's feet
are the god we love.
To meditate on the guru's feet
is true meditation.
Whoever touches the guru's feet
crosses over to the other side.
The guru's feet
are dearer than life.

मनसा वाचा और कर्म ना
गुरु के चरण प्रेम चित धरना।
गुरु के चरण होय सो होना,
हानि, लाभ, कै, दुख सुख मरना॥

रणजीत गुरु जी चरण तुम्हारे,
जीवन प्राण अधार हमारे।
गुरु के चरण मुक्ति फल दायक,
सहजो गुरु के चरण सहायक॥

18 ॥गुरु चरणों का महत्व॥

गुरु पग निश्चय परसिये, गुरु पग हिरदय राख,
सहजो गुरु पग ध्यान कर, गुरु बिन और न भाख॥

I offer him my mind, words and deeds,
as I lovingly lay my head at his feet.
Whatever happens at the guru's feet
    happens.
Why worry about profit and loss,
joy and sorrow,
    or even death?

Your feet, Ranjit guruji,
are our soul, our life, our foundation,
your feet offer us the fruits of liberation,
Sahajo says:
    the guru's feet
    always help us.

18 *The Importance of the Guru's Feet*

Touch the guru's feet,
keep them in your heart.
Sahajo says:
    meditate on the guru's feet,
    and speak of nothing else.

19 ॥चौपाई॥

गुरु के चरण कंवल चित राखूं,
आठ सिद्धि नव निधि हूं नाखूं।
सकल पदारथ गुरु पग माहीं,
गुरु पग पर से सब दुख जाईं॥

गति, मति, पलटे गुरु पग परसे,
गुरु पग परसे त्रिभुवन दरसे।
गुरु पग परसे ब्रह्म विचारे,
गुरु पग परसे माया छारे॥

गुरु पग परसे योग युगंता,
गुरु पग परसे जीवन मुक्ता।
गुरु पग परसे बंधन छूटे,
मोह ममता की फांसी टूटे॥

गुरु पग परसे हरि पद पावे,
होय अमर फिर गर्भ न आवे।
चरनदास पग महिमा भारी,
वार वार सहजो बलिहारी॥

19

I will keep the lotus-feet of the guru
in my mind,
caring nothing for the eight siddhis
or the nine treasures.
All objects exist
at the guru's feet.
All sorrows cease
on touching the guru's feet.

Backwards, forwards,
all inclinations are overturned,
on touching the guru's feet.
The three worlds become visible,
on touching the guru's feet.
One meditates on Brahma,
on touching the guru's feet.
Maya is turned to ash,
on touching the guru's feet.

One is endowed with yoga,
on touching the guru's feet.
One becomes liberated while still alive,
on touching the guru's feet.
All ties are broken,
on touching the guru's feet.
The bonds of attachment
and possession
are broken.
One falls at Hari's feet,
on touching the guru's feet.
One is immortal,
and will never enter the womb again.
The glory of Charandas's feet
is great.
Again and again
Sahajo
sacrifices herself
at his feet.

20 ॥दोहा॥

गुरु आज्ञा दृढ़ कर गहे, गुरु मत सहजो चाल।
रोम-रोम गुरु को रटे, सो शिष होय निहाल॥

21 ॥चौपाई॥

गुरु की आज्ञा दृढ़ कर गहिए,
गुरु की आज्ञा में नित रहिए।
गुरु आज्ञा बिन काज न कीजे,
हानि होय तो होने दीजे॥

गुरु की आज्ञा विघ्न न कोई,
गुरु की आज्ञा गुरु मुख होई।
गुरु की आज्ञा भक्ति बढ़ावे,
गुरु की आज्ञा पार लगावे॥

गुरु की आज्ञा सकल शिरोमणि,
गुरु की आज्ञा चले सो हरिजन।
गुरु आज्ञा माने सोई साधू,
गुरु आज्ञा का भेद अगाधू॥

20

When the disciple holds the guru's hand
and obeys his every command,
Sahajo says:
he walks the way the guru walks.

When the disciple chants the guru's name,
and every hair on his body stands erect,
he lives in ecstasy.

21

Hold firm
 to the guru's command,
Live each day
 according to the guru's command.
Do nothing
 outside the guru's command,
If you lose everything as a result,
 let it go.

The guru's command
 should not be resisted.
The guru's command
 comes from the guru's mouth.
The guru's command
 creates devotion,
The guru's command
 will take you across the ocean of existence.

The guru's command
 is the jewel on the crown.
The guru's command
 is the path of those born of Hari.
The guru's command
 properly followed
 makes one a sadhu.
The guru's command
 is an unfathomable secret.

जो कोई गुरु की आज्ञा भूले,
वार वार चौरासी झूले।
चरण दास गुरु आज्ञा पूरी,
बिन आज्ञा करनी सब कूरी॥

आज्ञा कारी गुरु मुख नीके
सहजो लोक भोग सब फीके॥

22 ॥गुरु निन्दक लक्षण॥

॥दोहा॥

गुरु आज्ञा माने नहीं गुरु ही लगावें दोष।
गुरु निंदक जगमें दुखी मुए न पावें मोष॥

23 ॥चौपाई॥

ऐसो का दरशन नहिं कीजे,
चरचा बात गोष्टि, तज दीजे।
उनका संग करे जो कोई,
वेमुख, निगुरा निंदक होई॥

Whoever forgets
the guru's command
will be reborn
eighty-four lakh times,
again and again.
The commands
of Charandas,
my guru,
are perfect.
Without his word
nothing I do
has any worth.

All will be well with him
who obeys the words
which come from the guru's mouth.
Sahajo says:
the disciple will find
that all worldly pleasures mean nothing.

22 *Characteristics of Those who Blaspheme the Guru*

Those who disobey the guru's command,
and blame him at every turn,
will find no happiness in this world,
and no salvation after death.

23

Do not seek the darshana of such a person.
Do not talk about them,
do not talk with them,
do not meet them.
Whoever keeps their company,
is stubborn,
a slanderer,
and has no guru.

गुरु दोषी की गति कहा गाऊं,
अपने मन ही कू समझाऊं।
उनकी चोरासी नहिं छूटे,
काल ज्वाल, यम दंड न टूटे॥

फिर फिर योनि संकट आवें,
गरभवास में अति दुख पावे।
जग में पात बबूला जैसे,
जीवत प्रेत निशाचर ऐसे॥

मन मैला तन सदा उदासी,
गल में डंभ कपट की फांसी।
सहजो तिनसे दूरहि भाजे,
नाम लेत मम रस ना लाजे॥

How can I sing
        of the man who slanders the guru?
I would rather avoid him.
Born eighty-four lakh times,
        he will never find release.
Surrounded by the flames of death
        Yama's clubs will beat him
        unceasingly.

Again and again
        he will suffer in the womb.
His stay in the womb
        will be a time of torment.
He will live like a leaf
        in the whirlwind of the world.
He will live like a ghost
        that walks abroad at night.

His mind will always be dirty,
        his body dejected.
Lies and deceit
        will hang like a rope around his neck.
Sahajo says:
        Run far away from him,
        far, far away!
My tongue is embarrassed
        to even talk of such people.

24 ॥दोहा॥

जो कुछ करै सो मनमुखी, मेटें गुरुमुख रीत।
वेद वचन समझे नहीं, चले चाल विपरीत॥

साधु कहावें जगत में, चलें दुष्ट की चाल।
डंभ भरे फूले फिरें, बहुत बजावें गाल॥

25 ॥चौपाई॥

वैमुख विषयी ज्ञान उचारें,
पांचों जीत, न मन को मारें।
दारा सुत को हरि गुरु जानें,
तन मन विषय वास लिपटाने॥

पाप पुण्य को झूंठ बतावें,
परनारी पर धन चित लावें।
महा अयोगी योग न जाने,
छल बल झूंठ कपट सिद्धि माने॥

24

Those who slander the guru
    are stubborn,
they erase the traditions
    which come from the guru's mouth.
They do not understand
    the words of the Vedas,
they walk away
    from dharma.

They may be called sadhus
    in the world,
but they walk
    in the ways of wickedness.
They strut about
    filled with pride,
    swollen with self-righteousness.
Their cheeks flap about,
    filled with hot air.

25

They are arrogant, sensual materialists,
    who boast of their own knowledge,
their mastery of the senses
    and their conquest of the mind.
Their wives and sons mean more to them
    than Hari and the guru.
Their minds and bodies
    are smeared with sensual desires.

They believe
    'sin' and 'merit' are lies.
They meditate
    on other men's wives,
    other men's wealth.
They are great masters
    of the yoga
    which is no yoga.
They manifest extraordinary powers
    of deceit, dishonesty,
    and hypocrisy.

साधु संत को ठगिया जाने,
राम भक्ति को तुच्छ बखाने।
ऐसे अपराधी बजमारे,
तृष्णा काम क्रोध के जारे॥

डूबे लोभ लहर के माहीं,
स्वपने क्षमा शील हिय नाहीं।
हिंसा अकस भरी मन माहीं,
मुख देखे नहिं सहजो बाई॥

26 ॥दोहा॥

गुरु वचन हिय में रखो, ज्यों किरपण के दाम,
भूमि गड़े माथे दिपें, सहजो त्यों हरिनाम॥

They think saints and holy persons
	are cheats.
They talk of devotion to Ram
	and call it worthless.
Indra's thunderbolts
	fall all around them.
They burn
	with desire, passion and anger.

They drown
	in the ocean of greed.
Even when they dream
	they cannot forgive others.
Their minds are filled
	with violence and envy.
Sahajo Bai says:
I will not look on their faces.

26

Hide the word of the guru
	in your heart,
the way the miser holds his treasure
	in the ground.

No matter
	how he hides it,
	his face will still shine.
Sahajo says:
	if you love Hari's name,
	the world will know.

27 ॥चौपाई॥

गुरु के शब्द हिए में धारे,
गुरु मुख गुरु के शब्द संभारे।
तीन लोक यम दूतन लूटे,
गुरु के शब्द बिना नहिं छूटे॥

मोह नींद में सब नर पागे,
गुरु के शब्द बिना नहिं जागे।
गुरु के शब्द शरण जो जावे,
छूटे कुबुधि परम गति पावे॥

गुरु के शब्द प्रेम उलझावें,
गुरु शब्द हरि आन मिलावें।
गुरु के शब्द जीव भ्रम नाशे,
गुरु के शब्द अभय पद भाषे॥

गुरु के शब्द राह नित चलना,
वेद पुराण कहा ले करना।
चरण दास गुरु शब्द तुम्हारे,
हमरे भरम फंद सब जारे॥

गुण सब गुरु के बचनों माहीं।
"सहजो" शिष सो बिसरे नाहीं॥

27

Wear the guru's words
in your heart.
Take care of the guru's words
they come from the guru's mouth.
Yama's messengers
pillage the three worlds;
without the guru's words
you cannot escape them.
All men are asleep
they live in delusion,
they drown in dreams.
Without the guru's words,
they will never wake up.
Whoever takes refuge
in the guru's words,
will be freed from foolishness
and find Supreme Bliss.

Entangle yourself in the love
contained in the guru's words.
The guru's words will force Hari
to come to you at once.
The guru's words destroy
all human illusions.
The guru's words speak
of freedom from fear.

Walk each day on the path
of the guru's words,
What need will you have then
for the Vedas and Puranas?

Guru Charandas,
your words
burn the ropes
which drag us here and there.
The guru's words remain firm
despite the changing qualities of the world.
Sahajo says:
the disciple
should never forget this.

28 ॥दोहा॥

शिष का माना सत गुरु, गुरु झिड़ के लखवार।
सहजो द्वार न छोड़िए, यही धारना धार॥

गुरु का दर्शन की जिए, गुरु का कीजे ध्यान।
गुरु की सेवा कीजिए, तजिए कुल अभिमान॥

सत गुरु दाता सर्व के, तू किरपण कंगाल।
गुरु महिमा जाने नहीं, फंस्यो मोह के जाल॥

गुरु सों कछु न दुराइये, गुरु सो झूंठ न बोल।
बुरी, भली, खोटी, खरी, गुरु आगे सब खोल॥

सहजो, गुरु रक्षा करें, मेटे सब दुख द्वंद।
मन की जाने सब गुरु, कहा छिपावे अंध॥

28

When you accept him
 as your true guru,
he may rebuke you a hundred thousand times,
Sahajo says:
 do not leave him.
Remember this always.

Take the guru's darshan,
 meditate on the guru,
serve the guru,
 abandon your pride in your family.
The true guru gives to all.
 If you are a miser,
 or a pauper,
you will remain trapped
 in the web of delusion,
and never know
 the glory of the guru.

Hide nothing from the guru,
 never tell him lies.
The good and the bad,
 the true and the false,
 are all revealed
in the presence of the guru.

Sahajo says:
 may the guru protect you,
 may he erase your sorrows
 and quieten your conflicts.
The guru knows
 everything that is in your mind.
The blind
 can hide nothing from him.

सहजो कारज जगत के, गुरु बिन पूरे नाहिं।
हरि तो गुरु बिन क्यों मिलें, समझ देख मन मांहि॥

परमेश्वर से गुरु बड़े, गावत वेद पुराण।
सहजो हरि के मुक्ति है, गुरु के घर भगवान॥

अष्टादश अस चार षट, पढ़ पढ़ अर्थ कराहिं।
भेद न पावे गुरु बिना, सहजो सब भर माहिं॥

सकल विकल सब छोड़कर, गुरु चरणन चितलाव।
'सहजो" निश्चय हरि जपो, बहुरि न ऐसो दाव॥

Sahajo says:
whatever you do in this world
will never be complete
without the guru.
How can you find Hari
without the guru?
How can you see Him
with your mind?
The guru is greater
than the Supreme Lord,
so sing the Vedas,
and the Puranas.

Sahajo says:
with Hari
there is liberation.
God dwells
in the guru's house.

You may read and read,
the eighteen Puranas,
the four Vedas
and the six Shastras,
and try to decipher them for yourself.
Without the guru
you will not crack open their secrets.
Sahajo says:
the scriptures will only deceive you
and lead you astray.

Give up all your resolutions,
your possible choices,
and bring your mind
to the guru's feet.
Sahajo says:
commit yourself
to chanting Hari's name.
You will not have
this chance again.

दीपक ले गुरु ज्ञान को, जगत अंधेरे मांहि।
काम, क्रोध, मोह, लोभ में, सहजो उलझे नांहि॥

सहजो गुरु परताप से, होय समंदर पार।
वेद अर्थ गूंगा कहे, वाणी केतिक बार॥

सहजो सत गुरु के मिले, भई और से और।
काग पलट भई हंस ही, पाई भूली ठौर॥

सहजो यह मन सिलगता, काम, क्रोध की आग।
भली भई गुरु ने दिया, शील, क्षमा का बाग॥

निश्चय यह मन डूबता, मोह लोभ की धार।
चरण दास सत गुरु मिले, सहजो लई उबार॥

ज्ञान दीप सत गुरु दियो, राखो काया कोट।
साजन वस दुर्जन भगे, निकस गया सब खोट॥

सहजो गुरु दीपक दियो, रोम रोम उजयार।
तीन लोक दृष्टा भई, मिटो भरम अंधियार॥

In the midst of the darkness of the world,
  take the lamp of the guru's knowledge.
Sahajo says:
    do not become entangled
    in desire, anger,
    delusion and greed.

Sahajo says:
    with the light of the guru's glory,
    you can cross the ocean of existence.
The mute can tell the meaning of the Vedas,
    over and over again.

Sahajo was transformed,
    when she met the true guru.
She had been a crow,
    she became a swan.
She remembered her true home.

Sahajo says:
    my mind smouldered with passion,
    with the fire of anger.
The guru made me good.
He placed virtue's yoke
    around my neck.

My mind was drowning
    in the river of attachment.
Somehow I found
    Charandas, the true guru,
    and he rescued me.

The true guru gave me
  the lamp of knowledge
  to light the fort
  of my body.
The good settled down,
    the evil ran away.
He removed
    all my faults.

सहजो गुरु दीपक दियो, नैना भए अनन्त।
आदि, अंत मध, एक हो, सूझ गए भगवंत॥

सहजो गुरु दीपक दियो, देखो आतम रूप।
तिमर गयो चांदन भयो, पायो परगट गूप॥

सहजो गुरु प्रसन्न हो, मेटे मन संदेह।
रोम रोम से प्रेम उठ, भीज गई सब देह॥

सहजो गुरु प्रसन्न हो, एक कह्यो पर संग।
तन, मन, से पलटी गई, रंगी प्रेम के रंग॥

The guru gave me
        the lamp of knowledge.
My whole body
        was illuminated.
I saw the three worlds.
The delusion of darkness
        disappeared.

The guru gave me
        the lamp of knowledge.
My eyes
        were eternal.
The beginning,
        middle and end,
        became one.
I saw
        God.
The guru gave me
        the lamp of knowledge.
I saw
        my self.
Darkness disappeared,
        the moonlight shone,
        the secret
        was made manifest.

Sahajo says:
        The guru was pleased.
        All doubts vanished from my mind.
Love arose from every pore,
my body was drenched.

Sahajo says:
        The guru was pleased.
        He told me a story about Hari.
My body and mind
        were completely overturned.
I was dyed
        in the colours of his love.

सहजो गुरु प्रसन्न हो, मूंद लिए दोऊ नैन।
फिर मोसे ऐसे कही, समझ लेहु यह सैन॥

सहजो गुरु कृपा करी, कहा कहूं मैं खोल।
रोम रोम, प्रफुलित भई, मुख नहि आवत बोल॥

चींटी जहां न चढ़ सके, सरसो ना ठहराय।
सहजो को वा देश में, सत गुरु दिया बसाय॥

सिख पौदा नौधा अमी, गुरु कृपा की बाढ़।
सहजो तरुवर फैल बढ़, सुफल फले यह झाड़॥

Sahajo says:
    The guru was pleased.
    He shut his eyes.
Then he hinted to me,
    do as I do.
The guru bestowed his grace on me.
How can I tell you what really happened?
My body was covered with delight,
my mouth was empty,
    there was nothing I could say.

Where the ant cannot climb,
    and the mustard seed cannot fit,
Sahajo says,
    the true guru placed me there,
    in that distant land.

The disciple is a sapling,
  watered with nine types of devotion,
and the flood of the guru's kindness.
Sahajo says:
    this worthless bush
    grew
    and bore good fruit.

29 ॥शिष्य के लक्षण॥

॥दोहा॥

सहजो शिष ऐसा भला, जैसे माटी मोय।
आपा सोंप कुम्हार को, जो कुछ होय सो होय॥

सहजो शिष ऐसा भला, जैसे चकई डोर।
गुरु फेरे त्योंही फिरे, त्यागे अपनी खोर॥

30 ॥गुरु लक्षण॥

॥दोहा॥

सहजो गुरु ऐसे मिले, जैसे धोबी होय।
दे दे साबुन ज्ञान का, कलि मल डारे धोय॥

सहजो गुरु ऐसे मिले, मेटे सब संदेह।
नीच ऊंच देखे नहीं, ज्यों बादल का मेह॥

सहजो गुरु ऐसे मिले, जैसे सूरज धूप।
सब जीवन को चांदना, कहा रंक कहा भूप॥

सहजो गुरु ऐसे मिले, समदृष्टी निर्लोभ।
शिष को प्रेम समुद्र में, कर दिया झोबा झोव॥

29 *The Characteristics of the True Disciple*

The true disciple
    is like well-worked clay;
he gives himself into the hands of the potter
and is
    transformed.

Sahajo says:
    the good disciple
    is like a toy on a string,
Whether the guru turns this way
    or that,
    he simply follows.
Such a disciple
    soon renounces
    all his ways.

30 *The Characteristics of the Guru*

Sahajo says:
    find a guru
    who will be like a washerman.
He will give you the soap of knowledge
    and wash away your sins.

Sahajo says:
    find a guru
    who can erase all your doubts.
He will be like the rain-cloud
    that does not distinguish
    between high and low.
Sahajo says:
    find a guru
    who shines like the sun.
He will illuminate all life,
    the prince
    and the pauper
    equally.
Sahajo says:
    find a guru
    who is impartial,
    and free from greed.

सहजो गुरु बहुत फिरे, ज्ञान, ध्यान, सुधि नाहिं।
तारि सके नहिं एक को, गहें बहुत की वाहि॥

ऐसे गुरु तो बहुत हैं, धूत धूत, धन लेहि।
सहजो सत गुरु जो मिले, मुक्ति धाम फल देहि॥

कुटुंब जाल जित तित, बिछो, पशु, पक्षी, नर, माहिं।
सहजो गुरु झिड़की बचे, निगुरा उलझत जाहिं॥

वार वार नाते मिलें, लख चौरासी माहिं।
सहजो सत गुरु ना मिले, पकरि निकासे बाहिं॥

जन्म-जन्म हरि संग ही, मिल रहे आठों याम।
सहजो गुरु के बिन मिले, पावे ना विश्राम॥

Be his disciple
    and drown,
    drown,
    in the ocean of his love.

Sahajo says:
    there are hordes of gurus
    wandering around,
ignorant men,
    who know nothing of meditation.
They reach out to many
    and cannot save any.
These gurus are common:
    cheats, villains,
    men who want your money.
Sahajo says:
    find a true guru,
who can give you the fruits
of the abode
    of liberation.

The web of the family
    is spread all about
among men,
    birds and animals
Sahajo says:
    the guru's rebuke can save you;
    without a guru
you will be entangled forever.
Eighty-four lakh times,
    again and again,
    they will find their relatives.
Sahajo says:
    the only safe way
    is to find the true guru.
Hari's company is available
    day after day,
    life after life.

Sahajo says:
    without knowing the guru,
    you will never have rest.

31 ॥अयोग्य शिष्य पर गुरु की असमर्थता॥

॥दोहा॥

सहजो गुरु पूरा मिले, शिष मैला घट चित्त ।
मेह बरसे कल्लर जमीं, खेत न उपजे छित्त ॥

मलयागिरि के निकट ही, सब द्रुम चंदन होहिं।
कीकर, शीशम, चीढ, तरु, हुए न कबहुँ होहिं॥

सिख माटी सिख पाथरा, सिख लकड़ी सम जोय।
सहजो गुरु पारस लगे, कैसे कंचन होय॥

शिष सराई तेल बिन, बाती भी नहिं माहिं।
सहजो गुरु दीपक मिले, चांदन होसी नाहिं॥

31 *The Inability of the Guru to Assist an Undeserving Disciple*

Sahajo says:
If the guru is good,
but mind and body of the disciple
are dirty,
it will be like rain
falling on a barren field,
nothing will grow.

Only sandalwood trees grow
near the Malaya mountain;
the acacia, shisham and pine
cannot grow there
and will never become fragrant.

When the disciple is clay,
stone, or wood, Sahajo says,
the touchstone guru may find him,
but he will never become gold.

When the disciple is a clay lamp,
with no oil
and no wick,
Sahajo says,
he may find
the shining lamp
but he will not
see the light.

सहजो गुरु समरथ कला, सर्व दर्शी सब अंग।
कोई कैसा शिष्य हो, सब ही हों प्रसन्न॥

सहजो गुरु रंगरेज सम, सब ही को रंग देत।
चाहे जैसा वसन हो, मैला, उजला स्वेत॥

सहजो गुरु दर्शन दिए, पूर रहे सब ठौर।
जहाँ तहाँ गुरु ही लखे, दृष्टि न आवे और॥

निरखत ही आनन्द भई, सत गुरु सरने जाय।
भवसागर दुख रूप से, सहजो लई बचाय॥

चरणदास के चरण पर, सहजो वारे प्राण।
जगत व्याधि से काढ़ि कर, दीनो पद निर्वाण॥

सहजो गुरु महिमा कही, पढ़ सुनि हियो सिराय।
उपजे गुरु की भक्ति दृढ़, दुविधा दुर्मति जाय॥

Nevertheless, says Sahajo,
when the guru is skilled
in the three arts,
        knowledge, devotion and yoga,
no matter what the disciple's condition may be,
all will be happy
when they take refuge in him.

Sahajo's guru is a dyer,
he colours us all with his dyes.
Whether our cloth be dirty,
shiny or white,
he dips it in his dye
and it comes out right.

Sahajo's guru gave her his darshan,
the whole world was hers.
She saw him everywhere she looked,
saw him and no one else.

On seeing him, she was filled with bliss.
She took refuge in the sat-guru.
He saved her from the sorrow
of the ocean of existence.

Sahajo lays down her life
at the feet of Charandas.
He plucked her out
        from the afflictions of the world,
and sat her down
        in nirvana.

Sahajo says:
        tell of the greatness of the guru.
        Read about him.
        Listen to stories of his life.
        It will refresh your heart.
May unwavering love for the guru
        be born in your heart.
May you be free
        from all evil inclinations.
May you never be confused.

32 ॥द्वादश प्रकार के संत बचन॥

मधुरी बोली, चट पटी बोली, अमृत बोली।
शीतल सुगंध बोली, सरल बोली, कोमल बोली॥
विघ्न विदारक बोली, भर्म निवारण बोली।
शुद्ध सुखसज्जन बोली, भक्ति दृढ़ावन बोली॥
स्थिर बोली, सांची बोली।

33 ॥द्वादश प्रकार के दुष्टों के बचन॥

पाहन बोली, कटु बोली, विष भुजंग बोली,
अग्नि स्वरूप बोली, अंकड़े खटक बोली, हिया
वेध बोली, तीव्र बोली, झूंठी बोली, निगुरी
बोली, छल कपट बोली, निदाप्रद बोली,
डिग मिगाट बोली।

34 ॥साधु महिमा का अंग॥

॥दोहा॥

साधु मिले गुरु पाइयां, मिट गये सब संदेह।
सहजो को सम हो गयो, कहा गिरिवर का ग्रेह॥

साधु मिले पूरी भई, जनम जनम की आस।
सहजो पायो भावतो, सत संगत में बास॥

32 *The Twelve Types of Holy Speech*

Sweet speech. Savoury speech.
  Speech of pure nectar.
Cool fragrant speech. Simple speech.
  Soft speech.

Speech that destroys all obstacles.
  Speech that wards off illusion.
The speech of the good, the pure and the happy.
  The speech that strengthens devotion.
Confident speech. Truthful speech.

33 *The Twelve Types of Wicked Speech*

Speech as hard as stone. Bitter speech.
  The speech of a poisonous snake.
Speech like fire. Clever speech.
  Cynical speech. Quick speech.
False speech. Speech without a guru.
  Deceitful, cunning speech.
Cruel speech. Uncertain speech.

34 *The Glory of the Saint*

To meet a saintly person
is to meet the guru.
  Both erase all your doubts.
Sahajo says:
  they are the same,
  even if one lives in a house
  and the other in the forest.

On meeting a holy person,
  the hope of many lives is fulfilled.
Sahajo says:
  I found what I desired,
  when I came into the community of the saints.

सहजो साधुन के मिले, मन भयो हरि के रूप।
चाह गई थिरता भई, रंक लखा सोई भूप॥

साधु मिले हरि ही मिले, मेरे मन परतीत।
सहजो सूरज धूप ज्यों, जल पाले की रीत॥

साधु मिले दुख सब गए, मंगल भया शरीर।
वचन सुनत ही मिट गई, जनम मरण की पीर॥

साधु संग में चाँदना, सकल अंधेरा और।
सहजो दुरलभ पाइए, सत संगत में ठौर॥

सत संगत की नाव में, मन दीजे नर नार।
टेक बली दृढ़ भक्ति की, सहजो उतर पार॥

Sahajo says:
    on finding a sadhu,
    the mind takes the form of Hari.
Desire departs,
the mind becomes stable,
one sees no difference
between a prince and a pauper.
To meet a holy person
is to meet Hari.
This is my firm conviction.
    Sahajo says:
    when the sun shines, the frost melts.

When I met the saint,
all my sorrows ceased,
my body became whole.
When I heard his words,
the pain of many births
and many deaths
came to an end.

There is moonlight
in sat-sang,
even though the rest of the world
is in darkness.
Sahajo says:
it is difficult to find a place
in the company of the saints.

Men and women,
place your trust
in the boat of sat-sang.
Use the powerful oar of devotion,
says Sahajo,
to take you to the other side.

35 ॥दोहा॥

साधु संग तीरथ बड़ो, तामें नीर विचार।
सहजो न्हाए पाइये, मुक्ति पदारथ चार॥

जो आवे सत संग ने, जाति वरण कुल खोय।
सहजो मैल कुचील जल, मिले सु गंगा होय॥

सहजो संगति साधु की, काग हंस हो जाय।
तज के भक्ष अभक्ष कूं, मोती चुग चुग खाय॥

जब चेते जब ही भला, मोह नींद से जाग।
साधों की संगति मिले, सहजो ऊंचे भाग॥

35

The company of the saints
is a great pilgrimage centre,
filled with the water of wisdom.
Sahajo says:
  Bathe there
  and you will find
  the four means of liberation.

In the company of the holy,
  whoever comes
  loses colour,
  caste and lineage.
Sahajo says:
  when polluted dirty water
  flows into the Ganges,
  it too becomes sacred.
Sahajo says:
    In the company of the wise,
    a crow becomes a swan.
Renouncing all distinction
    between the edible
    and the inedible,
    the crow
    eats fair and foul.
The swan
dines on pearls.

Whenever one finds awareness,
that is the right time
to wake from the delusion of sleep.
Sahajo says:
Sat-sanga is available
    only to those
    fortunate enough
    to discover it.

जो जन आवे शरण में, साधू ही दरसाय।
सहजो सांभर खेत में, गिरि सांभर हो जाय॥

सहजो संगति साधु की, भली मिली कुशलात।
नातर आवा गमन में, यम नित करता घात॥

सहजो संगति साधु की, छूटे सकल बियाध।
दुर्मति पाप रहै नहीं, लागै रंग अगाध॥

साधु वृक्ष वाणी कली, चरचा फूले फूल।
सहजो संगति बाग में, नाना फल रहे झूल॥

सहजो दर्शन साधु का, दो नैनों करि लेह।
तिहूं ताप नसि जांयगे, शीतल होगी देह॥

Whoever takes the shelter of a sadhu
becomes a sadhu himself.
Sahajo says:
    Near Sambhar salt-lake,
    even a mountain
    becomes Sambhar.

Sahajo says:
    In the company of the saints,
    one has the good fortune
    to find true virtue.
Otherwise
    one is born and reborn,
    and each day Yama
    seeks new victims.

Sahajo says:
    In the company of the holy,
    all afflictions fall away.
Evil inclinations and sins
disappear.
    The mind becomes
    a pure translucent lake.
Buds of speech,
flowers of discussion,
    grow on the sadhu-tree.
Sahajo says:
    in the garden
    of the company of truth,
the trees
    are covered with fruits.

Sahajo says:
    when you have the darshana of a saint,
    use both your eyes.
The sight
    will destroy your burning passions
    and cool your body.

सहजो दर्शन साधु का, देखूं वारूँ प्राण।
जिन की किरपा पाइये, निर्भय पद निर्वाण॥

36 दुष्ट लक्षण

दुष्टन की महिमा कहूं, सुनिये सँत सुजान।
ताना दे दे दृढ़ करे, भक्ति योग, अरु ज्ञान॥

37 ॥चौपाई॥

धन दुर्जन जो दृढ़ता देई,
निंदा कर पातक हर लेई।
दुर्जन, त्यागी देखे भारी,
समझ समझ सहजो बलिहारी॥

तज दिया साधु संग गुरु चरना,
त्यागी भक्ति ध्यान का धरना।
त्यागी उत्तम रहनी गहनी,
त्यागी हरि की लीला कहनी॥

Sahajo says:
    when you have the darshana of a saint,
    see truly
    and be prepared to lay down your life.

When he bestows his kindness upon you,
    all fear will flee
    and you will be worthy of nirvana.

36 *The Characteristics of the Wicked*

I will sing of the glory of the wicked,
    hear me, wise saints.
Through their taunting,
    they strengthen the pious
    in devotion, yoga and meditation.

37

Blessed are the wicked,
    who strengthen the saints in their faith.
When they slander us,
    we are freed from our sins.
The wicked are mighty renunciants.
When I realised this,
Sahajo says,
I devoted myself to their welfare.

They have renounced
    the company of the saints,
    the guru's feet,
    devotion, and meditation.
They have renounced
    the shelter
    of the best of all living creatures.
They have renounced
    the opportunity to hear about
    Hari's lila.

त्यागे वचन विमल सुख दाई,
तज दियो सांच झूंठ लौ लाई।
जत, सत, शील क्षमा तज दीना,
सो साधू माथे धर लीना॥

तजी दीनता सुबुद्धि चिताई,
सो गरीब साधो ने पाई।
तज वैराग्य परम संतोषा,
सब विधि तज्यो राम गति मोखा॥

38 ॥दोहा॥

भली चाल दुर्जन तजे, जैसा त्यागी होय।
बुरी चाल साधू तजे, तजन कहै सब कोय॥

They have renounced
 the holy words
 which give happiness.
They have abandoned
 any distinction
 between truth and falsehood,
 in the lies they tell.
They have abandoned
 truth, virtue and mercy.
The saints respectfully receive
 all the wicked leave them.

They have abandoned
 humility and wisdom,
leaving these qualities
 for the poor sadhu to find.
They have found supreme contentment
 in the renunciation of detachment.
They have renounced every way
 of finding Rama,
 the Lord of Liberation.

38

Like the renunciate,
 the wicked abandons
 conventional spiritual practices.
The sadhu abandons
 evil ways,
 and asks everyone else
 to do the same.

39 ॥साधु लक्षण॥

॥चौपाई॥

साधु सोई जो काया साधे,
तज आलस अरु वाद विवादे।
गहै धारणा सब गति धारी,
तजै विकलता स्तुति गारी॥

क्षमा वंत धीरज मन धारे,
पांचों बस कर मन को मारे।
त्यागे झूंठ सांच मुख बोले,
चित स्थिर इत उत नहिं डोले॥

तन जगमें मन हरि के पासा,
लोक भोग से सदा उदासा।
जत, सत, शील, क्षमा चितलाई,
तन मन वचन सबन सुखदाई॥

निर्गुण ध्यानी अरु ब्रह्म ज्ञानी,
मुख से बोले अमृत वाणी।
समझ एकता भाव न दूजे,
जिनके चरण सहजिया पूजे॥

39 *The Qualities of a Sadhu*

The sadhu
        practices sadhana.
He renounces sloth
        and foolish debates.
By focusing his awareness,
        he stills the changing patterns
        of the world.
He renounces distress,
prayer and insult.

One who knows forgiveness
is always patient.
By controlling the five senses,
        he kills the mind.
He renounces lies
        and always speaks the truth.
When his mind is stable,
        it does not run here and there.

With his body in the world,
        and his mind fixed on Hari,
he is indifferent
        to sensual pleasures.
His thoughts dwell
        on asceticism, truthfulness,
        virtue and mercy.
His body, mind and speech
        give joy to all.

He meditates on God-without-form,
        he knows Brahma.
His mouth is full
        of immortal words.
He understands the One,
        and has no other delight.
Little Sahajo
        worships
        his feet.

40 ॥दोहा॥

निर्द्वंदी, निर्वैरता, सहजो, अरु निर्वास।
संतोषी, निर्मल दशा, तकें न पर की आस॥

ज्ञान मध्य स्थिर सदा, ध्यान मध्य गल तान।
सहजो साधू राम के, तजें बड़ाई मान॥

जो सोवें तो शून्य में, जो जागे हरि नाम।
जो बोले तो हरि कथा, भक्ति करें निष्काम॥

तन मन मेटें खेद सब, तज उपाधि की चाल।
सहजो साधु राम के, तजें कनक अरु बाल॥

दीरघ बुधि जिन की महा, शील सदा ही नैन।
चेतनता हिरदय बसे, सहजो शीतल बैन॥

40

Non-dual,
at peace with all,
Sahajo says,
and free of passion.
Contented,
tranquil,
not dependent
on anyone else.

Established in knowledge,
firm in meditation,
Sahajo says:
the holy ones belong to Rama,
they have no pride,
they seek no praise.

When they sleep,
they rest in nothingness.
When they wake,
Hari's name is on their lips.
When they speak,
they tell stories of Hari.
When they sing God's praises,
they seek no reward.

Their bodies and minds
have no regrets.
They do not care
for the deceitful tricks of the world.
Sahajo says:
    the sadhus
    belong to Ram.
    They do not need
    gold or women.

They are men of vast wisdom,
whose eyes are filled with virtue.
Awareness abides in their hearts.
Sahajo says:
    their words
    bring great comfort.

तन को साधे ही रहें, चित को राखें हाथ।
सहजो मन को यों गहें, चलें इन्द्रिन साथ॥

नित ही प्रेम पगे रहें, छके रहें निज रूप।
समदृष्टि सहजो कहे, समझे रंक न भूप॥

सुरति नहीं ब्यवहार में, जगत रीति सूं पीठ।
सन्मुख है गुरु भक्ति में, सहजो हरि को ईठ॥

साधु कुसंगी सँग तजें, आतम ही को सँग।
बोध रूप आनन्द में, पियें "सहज" को रँग॥

दुर्जन ना सज्जन, नहीं, नहीं, वैर अरु प्रीति।
सकल विकल उनके नहीं, सहजो हरिजन रीति॥

They train their bodies continually,
they control their thoughts at all times.
Sahajo says:
they train their mind
not to follow the senses.

They live each day
filled with love.
They delight
in their own true form.
They see all men as equal,
says Sahajo,
no one is a pauper
and no one is a prince.

They live in awareness,
free of all actions.
They have turned their backs
on the ways of the world.
They face ever forwards,
filled with the love of the guru.
Sahajo says:
Hari is their friend.
The holy
abandon the company
of the wicked,
and associate
with their own true soul.
They find bliss
in awareness.
They drink
untainted
innocence.

They are neither good
nor bad.
They neither love
nor hate.
They make no choices.
Sahajo says:
the ways
of Hari's people
are simple.

सहजो हरिजन मुक्ति नित, डार दुई की पोट।
चाह गई शँसय मिटा, बँधन छूटे कोट॥

राग द्वेश से रहित नित, बैरागी, निर्द्वंद।
सहजो इच्छा ना रही, माया ब्रह्म की सँध॥

आसन सँयम साध करि, साधे प्राण अपान।
सहजो मुद्रा जो सधै, तौ योगी परमान॥

तीनों बँध लगाय कर, अनहद सुनै टकोर।
सहजो सुन्न समाधि में, नहीं साझ नहिं भोर॥

Sahajo says:
    Hari's people
    find their salvation daily
    by not taking up
    either of these two bundles:
they have no desires,
they have no doubts.
    In this way
    they are free
    of a million bonds.

Daily
    they neither love nor hate,
they live without attachment
    in non-duality.
Sahajo says:
    because they have no desires,
    they have reconciled
    maya and brahma.
They have disciplined the body,
    they have controlled
    the life-force and the down-breath.
Sahajo says:
    he who has mastered the mudras
    is a true yogi.

On applying the three
    internal muscular locks,
I hear the sound
    of the unstruck melody.
Sahajo says:
    at that moment
    I am in the samadhi of nothingness.
There is no evening.
There is no morning.

ना सुख विद्या के पढ़े, ना सुख वाद विवाद।
साधु सुखी सहजो कहे, लागे सुन्नि समाधि॥

मुए दुखी जीवत दुखी, दुखी भूख आहार।
साधु सुखी सहजो कहें, पायो नित्य विहार॥

चाह दुखी आशा दुखी, महा दुखी अज्ञान।
साधु सुखी सहजो कहे, पायो केवल ज्ञान॥

धनवंते सब ही दुखी, निर्धन हैं दुख रूप।
साधु सुखी सहजो कहे, पायो भेद अरूप॥

There is no happiness
    in knowledge,
    or in reading.
There is no happiness
    in debate.
The sadhu is happy,
Sahajo says,
when he enters
the samadhi of nothingness.

Death is full of sorrow,
    life is full of sorrow.
Hunger brings sorrow,
    so does food.
The sadhu is happy,
Sahajo says,
he knows eternal bliss.

Desire is full of sorrow,
    hope is full of sorrow.
The greatest sorrow
    is ignorance.
The sadhu is happy,
Sahajo says,
because he has true knowledge.

The rich are full of sorrow,
    the poor are sorrow incarnate.
The sadhu is happy,
Sahajo says,
because he has found
the secret of that
which has no form.

रंक दुखी राजा दुखी, दुखी सकल संसार।
साधु सुखी सहजो कहे, पायो भेद अपार॥

ना सुख दारा सुत महल, ना सुख भूप भए।
साधु सुखी सहजो कहे, तृष्णा रोग गए॥

The pauper is sad,
    the king is sad,
the whole world
    is full of sorrow.
The sadhu is happy,
Sahajo says,
because he has found the secret of that
which has no limit.

A wife will not make you happy.
A son cannot make you happy.
Becoming a king in a palace
will not make you happy.
The sadhu is happy,
Sahajo says,
because he feels no pain,
he has no desires.

41 ॥अथ वैराग्य उपजावन अँग वर्णन॥

॥दोहा॥

सहजो भजि हरि नाम को, तजो जगत से नेह।
अपना तो कोई है नहीं, अपनी सगी न देह॥

यही कही गुरु देव जी, यही पुकारे संत।
सहजो तजि या जगत को, तोहिं तजेगो अंत॥

कलह कल्पना दुख घना, सदा रहे मन भंग।
अकस हृदय से छाड़ि दे, सहजो जग बे ढंग॥

ज्यों संडासी लोह की, क्षण पानी क्षण आग।
ऐसे दुख सुख जगत का, सहजो तू मत पाग॥

अचरज जीवन जगत में, मरना निश्चय जान।
सहजो अवसर जात है, हरि सों करि पहिचान॥

PART 2: THE CULTIVATION OF DETACHMENT (VAIRAGYA)

41 *Now Begins the Description of the Cultivation of Detachment*

Sahajo says:
　　chant Hari's name.
　　Do not love the world.
No one belongs to you.
　　Not even your own body.

This is what guru-deva taught.
This is what all the saints teach.
Sahajo says:
　　Renounce the world.
　　One day it will abandon you.

The mind which is full of quarrel,
　　fantasy and sorrow,
　　will always be unfocused.
Remove envy from your heart.
Sahajo says:
There is no order in the world.

You live like a pair of tongs:
　　one moment in the water,
　　the next in the fire.
One moment you are happy in the world,
the next you are sad.
Sahajo says:
Do not become caught up
in whatever happens.
Life in the world
　　is unexpected.
Only death is certain.
Sahajo says:
Do not miss out on the opportunity
to make friends with Hari.

जग सेया जगमें पगा, जग संग दींने प्राण।
राम तज्यो जग सो रच्यो, सहजो निश्चय हान॥

झूंठा नाता जगत का, झूंठा है घर वास।
यह जग झूंठा देख कर, सहजो भई उदास॥

जब लग चावल धान में, तब लग उपजै आय।
जग छिल के कूं त्यागकर, मुक्ति रूप हो जाय॥

कुटुम्ब संघाती बीच में, आदि अंत नहिं कोय।
बीच मिले बिचही छुटे, सहजो संग न कोय॥

सहजो स्वास्थ सब सगे, दारा सुत अरु बीर।
जीवत जोते बैल ज्यों, मुए चढ़ावैं सीर॥

You are nurtured in the world,
        reared in the world,
and you will die in the world too.
If you abandon Ram,
        and create your own world,
Sahajo says,
you will lose everything.

Your relationship with the world is false.
Your life at home is false.
When I saw that the world was false,
Sahajo says,
I was filled with sorrow.

As long as there is rice in the husk,
one hopes for a rich crop.
Abandon the empty husk of the world,
and you will obtain salvation's essence.

The middle of your life
        is spent with family and friends.
When you are born
        and when you die,
you are alone.
Family and friends
        are not your true companions.
Sahajo says:
you meet them in the middle of life,
and lose them in the middle of life.
Sahajo says:
        relatives are a selfish lot,
        your wife, your son, your brother.
While you are alive
        you are bound to them
        like an ox to the plough.
When you are dead,
they will make offerings to you
to get what they want.

कोई किसी के सँग ना, रोग, मरण, दुख, बंध।
इतने पर अपना कहे, सहजो ये नर अंध॥

दरद, बटाय सके नहीं, मुए न चाले साथ।
सहजो क्यों कर आपने, सब नाते बर बाद॥

मर बिछुरे जब कुटुंब सो, बहुरन देखे आय।
महल दृव्य संतान को, सहजो पचै बलाय॥

मर बिछरन यों होय गो, ज्यों तरुवर सों पात।
सहजो काया प्राण ज्यों, ज्यों मुख सेती बात॥

No one cares about you
    when you are sick,
    when you die,
    when you are sad,
    when you are confined to your home.

Sahajo says:
    humans beings
    are blind.
You call them your own
but you cannot see
that they are not yours.

They cannot share your pain,
they cannot go with you when you die.
Sahajo says:
    you cannot call them your own,
    when they don't care about you.

When you die,
    you will leave your family
    and never see them again.
Your palace, your wealth, your children,
says Sahajo,
won't miss you at all.

Death
    is like a leaf
    falling from a tree.
Sahajo says:
    life slips out of the body,
    like words from the mouth.

सहजो जीवत सब सगे, मुए निकट नहिं जाहिं।
रोवें स्वारथ आपने, सपने देखि डराहिं॥

सहजो धन माँगे कुटुंब, गाड़ा धरा बताव।
जो कुछ है सो दे हमें, फिर पाछे मर जाव॥

मुख देखे ढापे भजें, तडदे तोड़े नेह॥
सहजो पति सुत, निज हितू, जार करें गे खेह॥

काढ काढ वेगी कहें, भीतर बाहर लोय।
जीव छुटे सहजो कहे, तेरा सगा न कोय॥

यह मंदिर यह नारि है, यह धन यह संतान।
तेरो ना सहजो कहे, काहे करति गुमान॥

Sahajo says:
Everyone wants you
    when you are alive,
no wants to go near you
    when you are dead.
They weep
    for themselves.
If they saw you again,
in a dream,
they would faint with fright.
Sahajo says:
your family wants your money,
even before you are dead.
"Whatever it is,
give it to us now,
then you can die whenever you please."

When they see your face,
    covered with a cloth,
    they will run away.
Their love
    will vanish in an instant.
Sahajo says:
    your husband, your sons
    your dearest friends,
will throw you onto the fire
and turn you to ash.
"Quick! Get it out!
Get it out of the house!"
say your family and neighbours.
When the soul has gone,
Sahajo says,
no one is your relative any more.

This temple,
    this woman,
this money,
    these children,
are not yours.
Sahajo says:
    why do you boast about them?

जन्म जुवा सम हार कर, किया न लाहा मूल।
डाल, पात, फल सींच कर, सहजो काटत मूल॥

सहजो गुरु परताप सो, ऐसी जान परी।
नहीं भरोसा स्वांस का, सन्मुख मौत खड़ी॥

भीतर का भीतर खुले, कै बाहर खुल जाय।
देह खेह हो जायगी, जै हो जनम गँवाय॥

स्वांसा दीपक के बुझे, होय अंधेरी देह।
सहजो सूनी प्राण बिन, फिर कैसो हरि नेह॥

सहजो फिर पछिताउगे, स्वांस निकस जब जाय।
जब लग रहे शरीर में, राम सुमिर, हरि गाय॥

स्वांस खजानो खटत निज, तनकहु सोधी नाहिं।
सहजो खरचो, का वच्यो, करि हिसाब घट माहिं॥

Life is a gamble
    you can not win.
You water the branches,
    the leaves and the fruit.
but neglect the roots.

Sahajo says:
    By the glory of the guru,
    I have learned
that you cannot trust life,
when death is your constant companion.

Your guts spill out,
your flesh cracks,
your body becomes ash.
Isn't that splendid!
How many lives
have you already wasted?

When the lamp of the breath is extinguished,
the whole body becomes dark.
Sahajo says:
    in death is misery.
    How can you love Hari then?

Sahajo says:
    you will repent
    with your dying breaths.
It is better
    to remember Ram now,
    to praise Hari
while you are still alive.
The breath rattles
    like a coin in a box
    and we never notice it.
Sahajo says:
    consider what you have spent
    and what remains,
    while you still are able.

सहजो नौबत स्वांस की, बाजत है दिन रैन।
मूरख सोवत है महा, चेतन कूं नाहिं चैन॥

हिरनाकुस से हो मिटे, दुर्योधन, शिशुपाल।
कुंभ करण रावण गए, सहजो खाए काल॥

निश्चय मरना सहजिया, जीवन की नहि आस।
कै टूटी हो झोंपड़ी, कै महलों में, वास॥

कै गरीब सिर टोकरी, कै सिर छत्तर होय।
जनम मरण में एक सम, सहजो भांति न दोय॥

मरना है रहना नहीं, जाना वाही ठोर।
सहजो के कंगाल हो, के हो दृव्य करोर॥

आप नहीं थिर होहिं जो, करें और को सोग।
सहजो साथी नाव के, सभी बटोही लोग॥

सभी बटोही बाट के, मिल, मिल, बिछरत जाहिं।
बैठि बैठि बहुतक गए, जग तरुवर की छाहिं॥

Sahajo says:
    the kettledrum of the breath
    plays on, night and day.
The great idiots sleep,
those who are awake
    worry all the time.
Hiranakusha lived
    and died.
Duryodhana, Shishupal,
Kumbhakarna, and Ravana
    all died.
Sahajo says:
death took them all.

Death is certain, Sahajiya,
there is nothing to hope for in life.
Whether you live in a broken hut
or reside in the palace of kings.

Whether you carry a basket on your head,
or walk daintily under a king's parasol,
Life and death treat all alike.
Sahajo says: we are all the same.

We all must die,
    no one remains.
Sahajo says:
    it makes no difference
whether we be destitute
or millionaires.

Those who are unsettled
    in their own heart,
grieve for others.
Sahajo says:
    we are strangers travelling together
    in the same boat.

We move in the same direction,
    we briefly meet
    and quickly part.
Together we all sit
    in the shade of this world,
    then separate
    forever.

यह रस्ता चलता रहे, थमें नहीं क्षण एक।
बहु आवें बहु जात हैं, सहजो आंखन देख॥

जग देखत तुम जाउगे, तुम देखत जग जाय।
सहजो यह ही रीति है, मत कर सोच उपाय॥

मुएमु काया जारि है, बहुरि न मिलि हैं आय।
रोय से कहा होति है, सहजो झुरे बलाय॥

झुरि झुरि के पिंजर भए, रोये गंवाए नैन।
मरे गए सो ना मिले, सहजो सुने न बैन॥

जो रोए से वाहुरे, तो रोवो दिन रात।
तन छीजे वह ना मिले, सहजो कूढ़ी बात॥

The path is endless
    and offers not one moment's rest.
Many come
    and many go.
Sahajo says:
    I have seen this
    with my own eyes.

You walk,
    wanting to see the world,
the world sees you.
Sahajo says:
this is how things are.
All your plans
    will come to nothing.

When you die,
your body will be burned,
you will never find it again.
Sahajo says:
    Why cry?
    Misfortune
    will destroy you.

Worrying
    will reduce you to a skeleton.
Crying
    will ruin your eyes.
Those who have died
    will not come back.
Sahajo says:
they cannot hear what you say.

If crying
    could bring them back,
then cry all you like.
No matter how hard you fret,
    they will not come back.
Sahajo says:
    it makes me sad
    to talk like this.

काहे को रोवत रहो, कलपत हो बे काजं।
सहजो गए सो जा चुके, आवें काल, न आज॥

देह निकट तेरे पड़ी, जीव अमर है नित्त।
दो में मूवा कौन सा, का सू तेरा हित्त॥

जो तेरा हित देह सूँ, नख सिख ताही खँड।
जीव अमर सहजो कहे, व्यापक और अखँड॥

तेरा था तो क्यों मुआ, गहि क्यों न राखा बाहिं।
सहजो बहुतक मिल छुटे, चौरासी के माहिं॥

कभूं कि तेरा बाप था, कभूं कि तेरा पूत।
कभूं कि तेरा मित्र था, कभूं कि तेरा सूत॥

Why do you keep crying?
It serves no purpose.
Sahajo says:
    the dead have gone
    and will not come back.
    Not today.
    Not tomorrow.

The body is in front of you,
the soul is immortal.
Which one dies?
Which one
    matters most?

If you are interested in the body,
    each part changes
    from top to toe.
Only the soul is immortal,
    Sahajo says:
it pervades the body
and is indivisible.

If she was yours,
    why did she die?
Why couldn't you protect her
    forever?
Sahajo says:
    many come
    and many go.
Each of us is born
    eighty-four lakh times.

Once
    he was your father.
Once
    he was your son.
Once
    he was your friend.
Once
    he was your enemy.

जो वाके सँग प्यार था, जाता वाके साथ।
कै वाही कू राखता, सहजो गहि कर हाथ॥

कलप रोय पछितावोगे, नेह तजोगे कूर।
पहले ही से जो तजे, सहजो साँवत सूर॥

यों खाता यों सोवता, मीठे कहता बोल।
यह विचार तू मति करै, चित होय डाँवा डोल॥

बैठ पहरि यों चालता, वस्तर भूषन लाल।
यह विचार तू मति करै, छल रूपी जग जाल॥

आगे रो रो क्या किया, अब क्यों रोवे भाँड।
सँग न आया ना चले, यह जग झूँठा माड॥

If you loved him,
    you should have gone with him.
Or taken his hand,
    Sahajo says,
    and kept him here.

One day you will be sorry,
    you will cry and weep.
One day you will regret
    you loved so much.
If you could renounce
    your attachments
    now,
Sahajo says,
you would be a brave warrior.

"I want to eat this,
I want to sleep there,
I want to say sweet words ..."
Don't think about those things.
The mind is fickle.

"I want to sit like that,
I want to walk around the sacred fire,
I want to wear a red sari
and ornaments of gold ..."
Don't think about these things.
The world is a web
woven with lies.

When you were a child,
    you cried and cried,
    to no avail.
Now you are an adult,
    your weeping
    is merely a game.
You came alone
and will die alone.
The world is false,
this cannot be denied.

आगे मुए सो जा चुके, तू भी रहे न कोय।
सहजो पर को क्या झुरे, आपन ही को रोय॥

बहुत गई थोड़ी रही, यह भी रहसी नाहिं।
जन्म जाय हरिभक्ति बिन, सहजो सुमिरन माहिं॥

उपजि, उपजि, फिर फिर मरे, यम दे दारुण दुःख।
लाज नहीं सहजो कहे, थिरग तुम्हारो मुख॥

पशु पक्षी नर सुर असुर, थिर चर कीट पतंग।
सब की उतपत्ति कर्म सों, सहजो नाना अंग॥

करमन के प्रेरे फिरो, जनम-जनम दुख होय।
मुक्ति विचारो सहजिया, आवा गमन जु खोय॥

Many have died.
They have gone,
    you will not live forever.
Sahajo says:
    why weep for strangers?
    Weep for yourself.
Many have died.
A few remain.
    They too will not live forever.
If you spend your life
    without devotion to Hari,
Sahajo says:
    you will have lived
    like a fool.

To be born
    again and again,
    and then to die,
is to suffer increasingly
Yama's cruel ways.
If you feel no shame,
Sahajo says,
a curse on your face.

Animals and birds,
humans, gods and demons,
movable creatures,
immovable creatures,
insects and grasshoppers,
are all shaped by karma.
Sahajo says:
it manifests itself in many forms.

If you follow your inclinations,
you will suffer each time you are born.
If you meditate on liberation,
Sahajiya says:
the cycle of birth and death
will come to an end.

जन्म चलो ही जात है, तनकहु सोची नाहिं।
जीवत जग्गह ना करी, बैठोगे किह ठाहिं॥

सहजो जैसी भावना, वैसी पावै ठौर।
जहां आस तहां वास है, निश्चय करी करोर॥

देह छुटे मन में रहे, सहजो, जैसी आस।
पुनर जन्म वैसा मिले, वैसे ही घर बास॥

42 ॥पूर्व जन्म वर्णन॥
॥चौपाई॥

जाकी रहे आस मंदिर में,
होकर घूंस बसे सो घर में।
रहे वासना द्रब्य मँझारा,
जन्मे नाग करे फुंकारा॥

रहे बासना तिरिया मांही,
कोटी स्वान धरे तन आई।
रहे वासना पुरुषा वर की,
कुतिया होय जु चुहड़े घर की॥

You are born
        and soon die,
without ever thinking.
If you do not prepare yourself now,
where will you be in your next life?

Sahajo says:
        you will be
        where your heart wants to be.
Your hopes
        will build your next home.
You have done this
        millions of times before.

The body dies
        the mind continues.
Sahajo says:
        what you hope for
        will determine your next birth.
What you hope for
        will build your next home.

42 *On Past Lives*

If you want to live in a temple,
        you may be born a rat
        and live in a house.
If you want to have lots of money,
        you may be born a cobra,
        hissing around a box.

If you want to be surrounded by fair women,
        you may be born
        from the womb of a dog.
If you want to keep company with many men,
        you may be born a bitch
        in the house of an untouchable.

जाकी रहे पूत में आसा,
सूवर जन्म नीच घर बासा।
जाका मन रहे राज द्वारा,
हस्ती हो सिर में ले छारा॥

रहे वासना नीर पियासी,
मीन देह धरि जल की वासी।
रहे वासना वाहन संगा,
पुनर्जन्म होय वाहन अंगा॥

जहां वासना जित ही जाई,
यह मत वेद पुराणन गाई।
चरणदास गुरु मोहि बताई,
तजो वासना सहजो बाई॥

43 ॥दोहा॥

सहजो लोक परलोक की, नहिं वासना ताय।
सो वह ब्रह्म स्वरूप है, सागर लहर समाय॥

जाकी गुरु में वासना, सो पावै भगवान।
सहजो चौथे पद बसे, गावत वेद पुराण॥

परमेश्वर की वासना, अंत समय मन माहिं।
तन छूटे हरि सूँ मिले, उपजे विनसै नाहिं॥

If you want lots of sons,
you may be born a pig
and live in a filthy hovel.
If you want to live at the king's door,
you may be born an elephant,
with dust on your head.

If you are always thirsty and want to drink lots of water,
you may be born a fish
and live in a river.
If you want to ride in a huge chariot,
you may be born with the body of a horse.

Where your heart wants to be,
there you will be.
The Vedas and Puranas teach this truth.
Charandas, my guru, told me once:
Renounce all desires,
Sahajo Bai.

43

Sahajo says:
He is the form of Brahma
who neither desires
this world or the next.

When your desire
rests in the guru,
you will find God.
Sahajo says:
Live in the fourth stage.
This is the message
of the Vedas and Puranas.

If the mind's desire
at the moment of death
is fixed on the Supreme Lord,
you will leave the body
and meet with Hari.
You will never be born again.
You will never die.

साधु संग की वासना, जिह घट पूरी होय।
मनुष जनम सतसंग मिल, भक्ति प्रापत होय॥

सहजो हरि के नामकी, रहे वासना बीर।
चौरासी संकट कटें, यम की छूटे पीर॥

चौरासी भटकत फिरी, दुख सहे नाना त्रास।
भव बंधन क्षण में कटे, चरण दास की आस॥

चौरासी के त्रास सुनि, यम किंकर की मार।
सहजो आई गुरु शरण, सुमिरौ सिरजन हार॥

धन यौवन सुख संपदा, बादर की सी छाहिं।
सहजो आखिर मरण है, चौरासी के माहिं॥

चौरासी योनि भुगत, पायो मनुष शरीर।
सहजो चूके भक्ति बिन, फिर चौरासी पीर॥

If body's desire
to live in the company of sadhus
is fulfilled,
you will take a human birth again
in your next life,
the company of holy ones,
will teach you devotion.

Sahajo says:
If you desire to dwell in Hari's name,
you will become a warrior.
You will escape the difficulties
of eighty-four lakh births.
You will not suffer
Yama's pain.

I wandered lost
in eighty-four lakh births,
I suffered great pain
and many sorts of terror.
The ties of the world
were cut in a moment,
when I met Charandas,
my hope and support.

I heard of the terrors
of eighty-four lakh births,
I heard how Yama's
messengers beat people.
Sahajo took refuge
in the guru.
I remembered
my Creator.

Wealth, youth,
happiness, and prosperity,
all pass
like the shadow of a cloud.
Sahajo says:
we are born eighty-four lakh times,
and die each time.

44 ॥उत्पत्ति व मरण प्रसंग वर्णन॥

॥दोहा॥

जनम मरण अब कहत हूं, कहूं अवस्था चार।
चौरासी यम दंड को, भिन्न भिन्न विस्तार॥

चरण दास आज्ञा दई, सहजो परगट गाय।
जाकूं पढ़ मुनि जीव की, सकल व्याधि कट जाय॥

45 ॥चौपाई॥

पापी जीव गर्भ जब आवे,
भवन अंधेरे अति दुख पावे।
तल मुंडी ऊपर को पाऊं,
मुख लंगी अरु भिष्टा ठाऊं॥

After eighty-four lakh births
in all sorts of bodies,
we found a human form at last.
Sahajo says:
If you miss out on bhakti,
you will have to endure
another eighty-four lakh births.

44 *Of Birth and Death*

Now let me speak
of the four stages
of birth and death.
Yama wields eighty-four lakh clubs.
I will speak of each stage
separately.

Charandas told me:
"Sahajo,
reveal in your songs, those things which
when read or when heard
will help human beings
escape their afflictions."

45

When the sinner enters the womb,
he is confined to a dark room
where he suffers great pains.
With his bottom up
and his shaven head down,
He lives with his face
between excrement and urine.

जठर अग्नि इक रस जहां लागी,
अधिक तपै जहां पतित अभागी।
खट्टा मीठा माता खावे,
लगै छुरी सी बहु दुख पावे॥

आप दुखी माता दुख पाया,
दसैं महीने जग में आया।
जग जंजाल देखि कर रोया,
नर नारी मिल सभी भलोया॥

माया मोह, पवन लग भूला,
सहजो गोद पालने झूला।
नाते सभी लगे जग झूठे,
पड़ा बंध में कैसे छूटे॥

46 ॥दोहा॥

सब नाते जनमत लगे, रोम रोम लिया बंध।
सहजो यह भी रल मिला, फिर फिर भूला अंध॥

Once lit,
    the fires of the stomach
    are never extinguished.
When the food is too hot,
    the baby suffers.
Sweet foods,
sour foods,
    cut like a knife.
The child suffers
    in so many ways.

For ten long months,
    the baby is sad
    and the mother is sad,
then he enters the world.
As soon as he sees where he is,
    he cries.
But when he meets mummy and daddy
    all is forgotten.

Once he is attached
    to Maya
    and life,
all is forgotten.
Sahajo says:
    when the baby plays
    in its mother's lap,
the false relationships of the world
close around him.
He is trapped in its bonds.
How can he escape?

46

On being born,
    relationships cling
    to every pore of your body.
Sahajo says:
    They become such friends
    that the blind man
    forgets everything
    again and again.

47 ॥नाते रिश्तेदारी वर्णन॥

॥चौपाई॥

कोई कहै मैं इस की माई,
कोई कहै लाला की दाई।
कोई कहै यह पोता बाला,
कोई कहै यह मेरा साला॥

कोई कहै यह सुन्दर हीरा,
गोद खिलाऊं अपना बीरा।
कोई कहै मैं याका बापू,
बालक पाया पुण्य प्रतापू॥

कोई कहै मैं याकी भूवा,
चाचा कहै भतीजा हूआ।
कोई कहै यह मेरा भाई,
कोई कहै मैं दादी आई॥

कोई कहै मैं याकी बहनी,
कोई कहै मैं याकी नानी।
कोई कहै मैं इसका मामा,
लाया खांड कडूले जामा॥

कोई कहै मैं इसका नाना,
मामी ने भानज कर माना॥

47 *Relationships*

Someone says:
  I am his mother.
Someone says:
  I am the wet nurse
  of this precious young lord.
Someone says:
  I am his grandfather.
Someone says:
  I am his brother-in-law.

Someone says:
  this bright shining diamond
  plays in my lap,
  he is my son.
Someone says:
  by my merits,
  I am the father
  of this child.

Someone says:
  I am his paternal aunt.
Someone says:
  I am his paternal uncle.
Someone says:
  I am his brother.
Someone says:
  I am his paternal grandmother.

Someone says:
  I am his sister.
Someone says:
  I am his maternal grandmother.
Someone says:
  I am his maternal uncle,
  and will bring him sweets,
  bracelets and a suit of pyjamas.

Someone says:
  I am his maternal grandfather.
Someone says:
  I am his maternal aunt,
  he is my nephew.

48 ॥दोहा॥

सब नाते लिए मान कर, घेरा घेरी घेर॥
झूंठे सांचे से लगे, सपने कंचन मेर।

पित्तर देवत, गोतिया, ग्रह नक्षत्र अरु सौन।
सहजो बंधन बंध गए, ताहि छुड़ावे कौन॥

49 ॥बाल्यावस्था वर्णन॥

॥चौपाई॥

गूंगा घी कहने जब सीखा,
सेढ्ढ नाम मदारी भीखा।
माय बाप, ले नाम पुकारें,
जब किलकै तब तन मन वारे॥

मुख चूमे अरु कंठ लगावे,
देवी देवा बहुत मनावें।
रोग होय तो बहु दुख पावें,
ले ले जहां तहां पग धावें॥

48

Having accepted all these relationships
he is surrounded by people,
surrounded by people,
surrounded.
The false seems true,
like a golden mountain
in a dream.

The ancestors, gods, kinsmen,
planets and heavenly bodies,
the worship of Shravana Kumar,
Sahajo says:
the bonds have been tied,
who can release him?

49 *Description of Childhood*

At first
the child is dumb.
Then
he learns to say "goo-ga".
His parents call him
"Sedhu", "Madari" or "Bhikha".
His mother and father
teach him his name.
They will sacrifice everything,
body and mind,
when he gurgles.

They kiss him on the face
and cuddle him.
They pray to many gods
and goddesses.
When he is sick,
they are very miserable,
and walk with him
to every shrine they can find.

कबहुं झड़प नजर लगि जावै,
कबहुं खांसी बहुत सतावै।
चले पेट कबहुं बहु रोवै,
खीझे बहुत नैक नहिं सोवै॥

ज्वर कबहूं दूखे दोऊ नैना,
बार बार दुख लहै न चैना।
निकसें दांत डाढ़ दुख दइया।
जब से जन्म सदा दुख पइया॥

50 ॥दोहा॥

दुख सुख भर बढ़ने लगा, पांच वरष भई देह।
तब पढ़ने बैठाइया, अपनी विद्या लेह॥

Sometimes,
 people scold him.
Sometimes,
 the evil eye falls on him.
Sometimes,
 he coughs a lot.
Sometimes,
 his stomach is upset,
 and he cries a lot.
Sometimes,
 he is angry,
 and cannot sleep.

Sometimes,
 he has a fever.
Sometimes,
 his eyes are sore.
Many things make him cry.
He is always upset.
When his teeth come,
 he cries.
From the moment he is born,
 he suffers.

50

Filled with sorrow and joy,
 he begins to grow.
When he is five,
 it is time to sit still
 and study,
 time for school.

51 ॥चौपाई॥

बालक का चित खेल मंझारे,
ज्यों ज्यों पाधा छड़ियन मारे।
बैठि रहे तो पकरि बुलावे,
बांधि बांधि दुख देत पढ़ावे॥

मन ही मन सोचे दुख भारी,
दुर्जन लगें बाप महतारी।
दुख दे दे कर बहुत पढ़ाया,
खोट कपट में घना सधाया॥

ऐसे भया बरस द्वादश का,
रहा नहीं उनहूं के बस का।
मन में आवे सो पुनि कर ही,
माता पिता से नैक न डर ही॥

खेले खेल बहुत परकारा,
सब ही विधि लड़कापन हारा।
बालपना हंस खेल गंवाया,
गुरु की टहल शरण नहिं आया॥

पाप पुण्य को नहिं पहिचाना,
सहजो कर्ता राम न जाना॥

51

The more he wants to play,
        the more the teacher
        beats him with a stick.
If he sits quietly,
        the teacher drags him
        to his feet
and ties him up.
The schoolmaster teaches him
        sorrow and pain.

His mind is full of misery.
His mother and his father
        are his worst enemies.
They send him to school
        to learn sorrow and pain,
and train him in fraud and deceit
        at his home.

Soon he is twelve,
        and impossible to control.
He does
        whatever comes into his mind.
He has no respect
        for his mother and father.
He plays all sorts of games,
like a child in every way.
His childhood has been lost
        in laughter and play.
He has failed
        to take shelter
        in the guru.

He cannot distinguish
        between sin and virtue.
Sahajo says:
        He does not know
        Ram,
        his Creator.

52 ॥युवावस्था वर्णन॥

॥दोहा॥

तरुणाया फिर आइ या, पांच भूत ले संग।
यौवन मद मातो फिरे, पिये विषय को रँग॥

53 ॥चौपाई॥

तरुणापा भया सकल शरीरा,
अंधा हुआ बिसरि हरि हीरा।
विषय वासना के मद मातो,
अहूँ आपदा के रंग रातो॥

मूंछ मरोड़ अकड़ता डोले,
काहूँ से नहिं मीठा बोले।
कहै बराबर मेरी नाहीं,
बुद्धिमान कोई या जग माहीं॥

मैं बलवंत सबन से भारी,
द्रव्य कमाऊं नरन अगारी।
महा दुखी सुख मान लियो है,
मोह अमल अज्ञान पियो है॥

52 *The Characteristics of Youth*

Carried along by the five elements:
desire, anger, pride,
greed and attachment,
he becomes a young man.
Intoxicated by the juices of adolescence,
he roams about,
drinking all the colours
of sensuality.

53

His body fully grown,
he becomes blind
and forgets
how precious Hari is.
He is intoxicated
by sensuality and passion.
His ego is coloured
by pride and selfishness.

He twirls his moustache
as he struts around,
and never speaks respectfully
to any one he meets.
He says:
"No one is as good as I am.
No one in the whole world
is as smart as me."
"No one can beat me in a fight.
No one earns more money than I do."
He lives in misery
and thinks he is happy.
He is drunk with the alcohol
of attachment and ignorance.

भया कुटुंबी फिर सुख कैसा,
सहजो बंद पड़ा कोई जैसा।
सुत पुत्री उपजै मर जावे,
सोच सोच तन मन दुख पावे॥

54 ॥दोहा॥

द्रव्य हीन भटकत फिरे, ज्यों सराय को स्वान।
झिड़क दियो जिह ढिंग गयो, सहजो रहो न मान॥

55 ॥चौपाई॥

द्रव्य हीन सबका मुख जोहै,
जाति वरण देखे नहिं कोहै।
निहुरि, निहुरि बंदर ज्यों नाचे,
राम तजो ग्रह बंधन राचे॥

बेटी ब्याह योग्य घर माहीं,
द्रव्य हीन कहु कित सों खाईं।
कहै हवेली एक बनाऊं,
अपने कुल में इज्जत पाऊं॥

Soon he is a family man.
    Now where is his joy?
Sahajo says:
    He lives
    like a man in a prison.
His sons and daughters are born,
    then they die.
His body and mind are worn out
    by constant worry.

54

Without money,
    he wanders about,
like a dog at a tavern –
    abused wherever he turns.
Sahajo says:
    Honour and respect
    do not remain.

55

Without any money,
    he must search each man's face
    carefully,
with no regard
    to colour and caste.
He bows to all,
    dancing
    like a monkey.
Having abandoned Ram,
    he is tied
    to his home.

He has a daughter at home,
    ready to be married.
He has no money
    for his family's food
But still he boasts:
    "One day I'll build
    a fine mansion.
Then everyone will respect us,
    for all that I've done."

कलपै बहुत सीस धुन माथा,
सहजो दुखी कुटुम्ब के साथा।
गयो नहीं सत संगति माहीं,
कुटुंब जाल छुटकारा नाहीं॥

हरि की भक्ति नहीं चित लाई,
दारा सुत धन की गुमराई।
दुख धंधा कर जन्म गंवाया,
सहजो सहज बुढ़ापा आया॥

56 ॥वृद्धावस्था वर्णन॥

॥दोहा॥

सहजो धौले आइयां, गिरने लागे दांत।
तन गुलझट पड़ने लगी, सूखन लागी आंत॥

He laments often,
        beating his brow.
Sahajo says:
        His family
        has brought him great sorrow.
        Because he abstains
        from the company of the true,
        he will find no release
        from their web.
He has paid no attention
        to the worship of Hari.
His wife, son and wealth
        have kindled his pride.
His life has been wasted,
        in the sorrow of work.
Sahajo says:
        old age comes easily
        to such a man.

56 *On Old Age*

Sahajo says:
His hair is white,
        his teeth are few,
his skin is wrinkled,
        his guts are shrivelled.

57 ॥चौपाई॥

डबडबाय आंखन में पानी,
बूढ़ेपन की यही निशानी।
नैनन में जल भरि भरि आवे,
दांत हले दारुण दुख पावे॥

गौड़े थके दर्द वाई का,
कफ़ खाँसी हिय दुख वाही का।
खों, खों, करे नींद नहिं आवे,
आप जगै अरु लोग जगावे॥

बेबस इन्द्री शिथल भई हैं,
अब क्या जीती सहज गई है।
पूत, बधू लखि नाक चढ़ावें,
बहुत पुकारें निकट न जावें॥

निहुर चलै लकड़ी ले हाथा,
"सहज" कुटुंब नहिं दुख के साथा।
असी बरस लगि बीते साठी,
सहजो कहै बहकि बुधि नाठी॥

57

When his eyes are filled to the brim
    with water,
this is a sign
    that old age has arrived.
The eyes fill with water
    again and again,
the teeth rattle
    and hurt when he eats.
Rheumatic pains
    attack his legs.
Coughing phlegm
    wearies the heart.
He coughs and he coughs
    but sleep doesn't come.
He stays awake
    and so does everyone else.

His senses are slack
    and hard to control.
Why does he bother
    to keep on living,
when he is already
    more dead than alive?
Each time his sons
    and daughters-in-law
    see him,
they turn up their noses.
He calls them to come,
    but they never do.

He walks bent over
    with a stick in his hand.
Sahajo says:
    his family
    have taken his possessions
    but will not share his misery.
He is eighty
    and senile.
Sahajo says:
    Old men babble.
    Their minds are worn out.

58 ॥दोहा॥

असी बरस ऊपर लगी, विरध अवस्था होय।
आगे की थिरता नहीं, पिछली सब गई खोय॥

तीन अवस्था बीत कर, चौथी आई मँद।
बृद्धावस्था सिर चढ़ी, तऊ न चेता अँध॥

59 ॥चौथी मरर्णासन्न अवस्था वर्णन॥

॥चौपाई॥

लागी विरध अवस्था चौथी,
सहजो आगे मौत हि मौती।
हाथ पैर सिर कांपन लागे,
नैन भए बिन ज्योति अभागे॥

श्रवणन से कछु सुनत जु नाहीं,
दांत डाढ़ नहिं मुख के माहीं॥

कंठ रुके कफ वायु घेरी,
हाड़ हाड़ सब दुख में पेरी।
बात कहै घर बाहर हांसो,
कुटुंब दियो मिल पौली बासो॥

58

Now he has reached eighty,
he is very old indeed.
His future is uncertain,
his life
has gone.

He has passed three stages,
and is far advanced in the fourth:
he is a silly old man!
Old age has conquered him
and still he has not woken up.
Still he is blind!

59 *The Stage of being at Death's Door*

Once the fourth stage,
old age, begins,
Sahajo says:
ahead of him is death,
only death.
His hands, feet and head
all begin to shake.
His wretched eyes
lack all light.

His ears hear nothing.
There are no teeth
in his mouth.
His throat is full of phlegm,
full of wind.
His bones grind painfully
against each other.
At home and away
people laugh at his words.
His family make him sleep
near the door.

मन चाले सब रस कूं तरसे,
नर नारी कोई हितू न दर से।
आप आप कूं इत उत डोलें,
बिन कारज मुखसे नहिं बोलें॥

जिन कारण पचिया दिन राती,
प्यार करे नहिं कुटुंब संघाती।
सुत पोते दुर्गंध घिनावें,
टहल करें तो नाक चढ़ावें॥

जिन के मोह तज्यो जगदीशा,
अब मन में कलपै धुनि शीसा।
चरणदास गुरु कही विशेषी,
गुरु बिन यों ही जाती देखी॥

60 ॥दोहा॥

सेत रोम सब हो गए, सूकन लागी देह।
सहजो वह मुख ना रहा, उड़ने लागी खेह॥

His mind wanders,
        longing for the good things
        he once knew.
No one, man or woman,
        seems to care about him,
he moves here and there
        alone.
Nothing he says
        seems to make any sense.

He worked hard, day and night,
        for their sake.
No one loves him,
        neither his family nor friends.
His sons and grandsons
        think he stinks.
        They hate him.
If they attend to his body,
        their faces are filled with disgust.

He abandoned the Lord of the universe
        for their sake.
His heart is full of sorrow,
        his mind is full of grief.
The Master, Charandas,
        said these important words:
This is how it goes
        without a guru.

60

His hair has turned white,
        his body has begun to wither.
Sahajo says:
        his face has changed.
Dust and disgrace
        have begun to blow about him.

सहजो इन्द्री सब थकी, तन पौरुष भयो छीन।
आशा, तृष्णा, ना मिटी, सहज वचन भए दीन॥

चार अवस्था खो दई, लियो न हरि को नाम।
तन छूटे यम कूट है, पहुंचे जब यम धाम॥

आय जगत में क्या किया, तन पाला कै पेट।
सहजो दिन धंधे गया, रैन गई सुख लेट॥

सहजो मृत्यु आइया, लेटा पांव पसार।
नैन फटे नारी छुटी, सौं ही रहा निहार॥

61 ॥चौपाई॥

पित सर का वायू घर आया,
वायु सरक कफ ठौर बसाया।
कफ़ सर का गल रोक लिया है,
कंठ रुके कोई नाहिं जिया है॥

Sahajo says:
 his senses are weak,
 his body is tired.
Only his hopes and desires
 remain unabated.
His words are humble.

The four stages have been wasted.
He never chanted Hari's name.
Ahead of him
 is Yama's abode.
When he leaves his body
that will be his home

What did he do
 when he reached the world?
He nurtured the body
 and fed the belly.
Sahajo says:
 he worked all day
 and slept all night.

Sahajo says:
 now death comes.
He will lie
 with his feet spread out,
His eyes open,
 pulse gone,
staring at the sky.

61

When the bile shifts
 and the humours take hold,
When the humours shift
 and settle where the phlegm should be,
When the phlegm shifts
 and blocks the throat,
When the throat is blocked,
 no one lives.

घुटर घुटर जब करने लागा,
चैतनता सब तनका भागा।
सकल कुटुंबी घिर घिर आए,
थोथा अपना नेह जताए॥

आंखन में जल भरि भरि लावें,
आपस में सब मोह दिखावें।
हाय हाय कोई कर बोले,
कोई ढूंढता औषधि डोले॥

कोई कहे कछु द्रव्य बताओ,
धरा ढका कुछ कर्ज दिखाओ।
वाको सुधि नहिं अपने तन की,
यम किंकर मारत है घन की॥

62 ॥दोहा॥

यम की सूरत देख कर, सुधि बुधि गई नसाय।
सहजो जो सँकट बन्यो, मुख सों कहो न जाय॥

सहजो मृत्यू के समय, पीड़ा होत अपार।
बीछू साठ हजार ज्यों, डँक लगे इक सार॥

When the death-rattles begin,
and consciousness starts to leave the body,
the relatives come and gather around,
to express their own hollow love.

Their eyes fill with tears,
as they express their affection,
        one to the other.
"Alas! Alas!" someone cries,
while another goes searching for medicine.

Someone says:
        "Do you have any money?
        Show us what you have,
        covered and kept,
        to pay your debts."
The old man
        loses consciousness
        of his body,
as Yama's servants
        beat him
        with thunderbolts.

62

On seeing Yama's face,
        the mind is destroyed.
Sahajo says:
        the awful pains one suffers
        cannot be described.

Sahajo says:
        the pains one suffers
        at the hour of death
        are endless.
They are like
        sixty-thousand scorpions
        stinging you,
        all at the same time.

63 ॥चौपाई॥

कोई कहे भज राम हि रामा,
सहजो कहे कौन अब कामा।
आगे से हरि सुमिरे नाहीं,
पचि पचि मुआ कुटुंब के माहीं॥

हिरदय रखता राम संघाती,
तौ रक्षा अब सब बनि आती।
आगे से अभ्यास जु रहता,
तो अब मुख से हरि हरि कहता॥

तन की पीड़ा सब मिटि जाती,
यम की तोपें कहा बसाती।
राम नाम मरते भी कहता,
जो आगे से कहता रहता॥

तै मन दिया कुटुंब के साथा,
हो बैठा अब दीन अंनाथा।
अपना किया भुगत रे जीया,
जो गुरु पूरा ढूंढ न कीया॥

63

Someone says:
    "Worship Ram,
    chant his name."
Sahajo says:
    what use is that now?
If you did not remember Hari
    while you were alive,
you will die in distress,
    surrounded by your family.

If you had kept Rama in your heart
    as your constant companion,
he would have protected you now.
If you had been constantly engaged
    in chanting His name,
your mouth would have called
    "Hari, Hari!"

The pains of your body
    would have been erased.
Where could Yama
    hide his cannons?
If Rama's name
    had been always on your lips
    while you were alive,
you would have called
    His name
    while you were dying.

You thought only of your family,
    now they are destitute,
    now they are orphans.
Oh soul,
    suffer the consequences of your actions.
You did not do
    the one thing you should have,
you did not search
    for the perfect master.

64 ॥दोहा॥

पकड़ बांध यम ले चला, धर्मराय के पास।
कई बार आगे गया, छप्पन जहां तिरास॥

कई भांति के डंड हैं, सहजो नाना त्रास।
नरक कुंड दुख भुगत कर, फिर चौरासी बास॥

65 ॥अकाल मृत्यु वर्णन॥

॥दोहा॥

अकाल मृत्यु अब कहत हूं, चौंक उठें अज्ञान।
समझेगा कोइ साधु जन, कै कोई विद्वान॥

जग विषयन की वासना, हरि सो नाहिं हेत।
अकाल मृत्यु कोई मरे, निश्चय होवे प्रेत॥

चार पहर का तेल भर, राखे दीवा बाल।
तेल निबड़ बाती बुझे, सहजो पूरा काल॥

64

Yama will grab you,
        tie you up,
        and take you to the Dharmaraj.
You have been there
        many times before
and have suffered
        each of the fifty-six forms of punishment.

There are many types of torture,
Sahajo says,
        very many indeed.
When you have finished
        with the pains
        of the pits of hell,
you will return to the round
        of eighty-four lakh wombs
        once again.

65 *Couplets Describing Untimely Death*

Now I shall speak
        of untimely death.
The ignorant will be frightened,
but saints and learned persons
        will understand me.

When someone who lives in the world
        follows sensual pleasures
        and has no love of Hari,
        dies a premature death,
he will become a ghost.

If you pass through all four stages of life,
        and your lamp is filled with oil,
        it will burn steadily
        until there is no more fuel.
Sahajo says:
        that is a full life.

कै मनुष्य कै वायु सू, कै पतंग कर देय।
तेल रहै बाती बुझे, अकाल मृत्यु कहि तेह॥

66 ॥चौपाई॥

बूढ़ा बाला या हो तरुना,
अकाल मृत्यु बिन काल जु मरना।
काल मृत्यु जो पहले गाई,
अकाल मृत्यु कहे सहजो बाई॥

शस्तर मौर मरे जो कोई,
यह भी मौत अकालई होई।
बिगड़े रोग पथ्य नहिं कीनो,
यह भी मौत अकालहि चीनो॥

किही भांति जो विष खा मरे,
अरु जीवत पावक में जरे।
जल में डूब जाय कोई कैसे,
लागे प्रेत मरै कोई ऐसे॥

But if a person, the wind,
        or a moth,
        extinguishes the flame
before the fuel is finished,
        that is
        a untimely death.

66

Whether you be old,
        a child or a youth,
if you die before you should,
        that is a premature death.
I have already sung
        of timely death.
Now Sahajo Bai will sing
        of untimely death.

If someone is killed by a weapon,
        that is a untimely death.
If someone becomes sick
        from following the wrong diet,
This too should be seen
        as a premature death.

Some die
        from eating poison.
Some
        are burnt in a fire
        while still alive.
Some, somehow,
        drown in water.
Those who die in these ways
        all become ghosts.

सांप डसै छूटे जो काया,
महलापतनी तें दबि जाया।
कोई ठग फांसी दे मारै,
जंगल पशू तोड़ जो डारे।

यह सब मृत्यु अकाल बताई,
मुऐ सु मौति पिशाचर पाई॥

67 ॥दोहा॥

प्रेत योनि को पाय के, दुखी हुए अज्ञान।
आप दुखी दुख देत हैं, उठ गई सब पहचान॥

68 ॥चौपाई॥

पेटं बड़ा मुख सुई समाना,
भूख प्यास में फिरे दिवाना।
भटकत फिरे ठौर नहिं पावे,
लगता फिरे जूतियां खावे॥

Some
　　are bitten by snakes.
Some
　　are buried when the walls fall down.
Some
　　are strangled by thugs.
Some
　　are torn apart by wild animals.

All these
　　are called
　　untimely death.
Those who die in this way
　　are born again
　　as ghostly demons.

67

Having obtained birth as a demon,
　　ignorant souls are miserable,
and, being miserable,
　　they inflict misery on others.
They do not care whom they hurt.

68

With a big stomach
　　and a mouth the size of a needle,
he wanders
　　crazed by hunger and thirst.
He wanders aimlessly,
　　provoking others,
wanders aimlessly,
　　thoroughly shamed.

बासा लहै कुचील ठिकाना,
आप कुचील कुचील ही बाना।
पाप करे हरि को बिसरावै,
सहजो कहे सो यह गति पावै॥

69 ॥नर्क वर्णन॥

॥दोहा॥

रही सु आयुर्दा कटै, मृत्यु लोक के माहिं।
जबही पूरी हो चुके, बाधे नर्कहि जाहिं॥

अति निकृष्ट वह ठौर है, महा घोर भय मान।
त्राहि त्राहि पापी करें, सुने न कानों कान॥

70 ॥चौपाई॥

बहुतक घोर नर्क में पड़े,
बहुतक थंभे बांधे ख़ड़े।
बहुतन के सिर आरे धरे,
कुंभी पाक नर्क अति पड़े॥

बहुतन के मुख सांप लगाए,
बहुतक पापी अग्नि तपाए।
बहुतों का सिर नीचा कीया,
ऊपर पांव बांध जो दीया॥

He lives in a dirty house.
    He is dirty.
    His clothes are dirty.
He sins,
    forgetting Hari.
Sahajo says:
    this is the death
    he deserves.

69 *Couplets describing Hell*

He lives that way for a long time
    in the mortal world.
When he has finished,
    he is tied up and taken to hell.

It is a wretched vile place,
    full of fear,
    I tell you true.
"Save me! Save me!" sinners cry out,
no one has ears
    to hear them at all.

70

Many people
    lie in darkest hell.
Many stand
    tied to pillars.
Many have saws
    placed on their heads.
Many lie
    in the darkest depths
    of Kumbhipak.

Many have snakes
    biting their faces.
Many sinners
    are roasted in fires.
Many hang
    upside down,
their feet
    tied with ropes.

तले कढ़ाई तेल जलाया,
भर भर कलछे छोंक लगाया।
बहुतक पकड़ कुंड में डारे,
जिन सिर कागा चौंचन मारें॥

कहां लग त्रास कहूं बहुतेरे,
छप्पन त्रास कहे गुरु मेरे।
यम घेरत है सकल मंझारी,
सब ही भुगतें नर क्या नारी॥

फिर फिर मुंडी जाय कुटावें,
सहजो कहे नहीं सकुचावें॥

71 ॥दोहा॥

यम का अधम शरीर है, पापी अधम शरीर।
जैसे को तैसा गहै, वैसी वाको पीर॥

त्रास दहन यम के कहे, सुन भगियो नर नार।
अब चौरासी कहत हूं, भिन्न भिन्न विस्तार॥

Many fry
    in cauldrons of oil,
basted
    again and again
    with big spoons.
Many are caught
    and put in pots.
Many have crows
    pecking at their heads.

There are so many punishments,
    how can I describe them all?
My guru told me
    there are fifty-six terrors.
Yama is everywhere
    and close to everyone.
They all suffer,
    men and women alike.

They are beaten about the head,
    time and time again.
Sahajo says:
    I have no hesitation
    in telling you this.

71

Yama has a vile body,
    a sinful, debased body.
He seizes sinners
    and punishes them as they deserve,
    tit for tat.

I have described
    the fierce flames
    of Yama's tortures.
Flee them,
    oh men and women.
Now I shall describe the eighty-four,
    with many different details.

72 ॥चौरासी लाख योनि वर्णन॥

॥चौपाई॥

नौलख जल के जीव बताए,
बहुत जन्म इनमें भुगताए।
पक्षी जाति कही दस लाखा,
आगे से चलि आई साषा॥

ग्यारहं लाख कृमि, कीट, लखाऊं,
जमीं माहिं जो चलत दिखाऊं।
बीस लाख थावर विस्तारा,
भर मत भर मत ही पचिहारा॥

तीस लाख पशु योनि सुनाया,
घनी बार जो भुगती काया।
चार लाख जो मानुष देही,
लख चौरासी यह सुन लेई॥

72 *A Description of the Eighty-four Lakh Births*

We are told
        that there are nine hundred thousand
        water creatures.
Each of us suffer
        many births in these forms.
It is said
        that there are ten lakh
        creatures which fly.
These are old numbers,
        set a long time ago.

There are eleven lakh
        worms and insects,
I see them
        moving in the earth.
There is the vast number
        of twenty lakh
        immovable creatures.
They have erred, they have erred,
and they live
        in distress.

I have been told
        that there are thirty lakh
        animal births.
We have suffered in these bodies
        many a time.
There are forty lakh
        human births.
Listen as I tell you
        of eighty-four lakh
        births.

इक इक बार सभी तुम भए,
कहिए कहां कहां दुख सहे।
दुख खे खे कर यह तन पाया,
सहजो हरि गुरु बिना गंवाया॥

चरणदास गुरु पूरे पाए,
चौरासी यम दंड छुड़ाए॥

॥इति वैराग्य उपजावन का अंग संपूर्ण॥

You have been born
in each of these forms
one after the other.
Tell me of the places
where you endured these sorrows.
Having suffered, having suffered,
you gained this body.
Sahajo says:
Unless you take refuge
in Hari and the guru,
the whole process is wasted.

I have found Charandas
The Perfect Master.
He has released me
from Yama's eight million
and four hundred thousand
punishments.

Here ends the Part of the Volume which is Intended to Arouse Detachment

73 ॥अथ नाम महात्म्य का अंग वर्णन॥

॥दोहा॥

लख चौरासी जो कही, बार बार भुगतंत।
जनम मरण छूटै नहीं, बिना शरण भगवंत॥

यज्ञ दान तीरथ करो, पूजा भांति अनेक।
मुक्ति न पावे सहजिया, बिना भक्ति हरि एक॥

इन्दर की पदवी मिले, अस ब्रह्मा की आय।
तौ भी निश्चय मरन है, सहजो हरि चित लाय॥

राम नाम ले सहजिया, तजिये सकल मरोड़।
तीन लोक के राजलो, अंत जाहुगे छोड़॥

PART 3: COMMITMENT TO TRUTH (SATYA VAIRAGYA)

73 *Couplets Describing the Glory of the Name of the Lord*

I have spoken
    of the eighty-four lakh,
    which we suffer again and again.
We will never be released
    from birth and death
    unless we take shelter
    in the Lord.

You may perform sacrifices,
    give alms,
    go on pilgrimages,
    worship in many ways,
but you will never be saved,
    Sahajiya,
without that one thing:
    devotion to Hari.

Even if you took
    the title of Indra,
and lived as long
    as Brahma,
one day
    you will still die.
Sahajo says:
Keep your mind fixed on Hari.

Chant the name of Ram,
    Sahajiya says.
Abandon all twists and turns.
Even if you were king of the three worlds,
one day
    you will have to leave them behind.

भक्ति बिना थोथे सभी, योग यज्ञ आचार।
राम नाम हिरदय धरो, सहजो यहि विचार॥

यह अवसर दुर्लभ मिला, पाई मनुषा देह।
लाभ यही सहजो कहे, हरि सुमिरण कर लेह॥

एक घड़ी का मोल ना, दिन का कहा बखान।
सहजो ताहि न खोइये, बिना भजन भगवान ॥

पारस "नाम" अमोल है, धनवँते घर होय।
परख नहीं कँगाल को, सहजो डारै खोय॥

सहजो जा घट नाम है, सो घट मंगल रूप।
नाम बिना धिक्कार है, सुन्दर धनवँत भूप॥

सहजो वाका नाम ले, गहि गहि उतरो पार।
राम सुमिर जानो नहीं, ते डूबे मँझधार॥

Without devotion,
even yoga, rituals and morality
are hollow.
Keep Rama's name in your heart,
Sahajo says,
think only of Him.

Having found a human body,
you have found a rare opportunity.
Sahajo speaks of the benefit
of always remembering Hari.

If even a few moments are precious,
what can one say of a whole day?
Sahajo says:
do not let a day pass,
without singing the praises of the Lord.

His Name is a touchstone,
beyond all price.
Those who have it are rich.
Those who do not appreciate it are poor,
says Sahajo,
and they quickly lose what they have.
Sahajo says:
the vessel that holds the Name
is auspicious.
Without it, one is cursed,
whether one be handsome,
wealthy, or even a king.

Sahajo says:
Take His Name,
hold on to it tightly
as you cross the ocean of existence.
Those who do not know
how to remember Ram
will drown
on the way.

सहजो भवसागर वहै, तिमिर बास घनघोर।
तामें नाम जहाज है, पार उतारे तोर॥

पावक नाम जलाय है, पाप ताप दुख द्वन्द।
राम सुमिर सहजो कहै, जो बिसरे सो अँध॥

कनक दान गजदान दे, उननचास भू दान।
निश्चय कर सहजो कहे, ना हरि नाम समान॥

मेह सहै सहजो कहै, सहै शीत अरु घाम।
पर्बत बैठो तप करे, तौभी अधि की नाम॥

चरण दास हरि नाम की, महिमा कही अपार।
सो सहजो हिरदय धरी, अचल धारना धार॥

सहजो सुमिरन कीजिये, हिरदय माहिं दुराय।
होट, होट सो ना मिले, सकै न कोई पाय॥

Sahajo says:
    a terrible darkness
    resides in the currents
    of the ocean of existence.
The Name is a ship
which will carry you safely across.

The Name is a purifying fire
    which destroys sin, passion,
    sorrow and conflict.
Remember Ram always.
Sahajo says:
Whoever forgets Him
    is blind.

You may give away gold,
    the gift of an elephant,
    or forty-nine pieces of land.
None of these,
says Sahajo,
is equal to Hari's Name.

The ascetic endures the rain,
says Sahajo,
the cold and the sun.
He sits on a mountain
doing penance,
But Hari's Name
is better by far.

Charandas said
that the glories of Hari's Name
are limitless.
Sahajo has placed
    the Name in her heart,
and carries it constantly
wherever she goes.

Sahajo says:
    when you chant the Name of Hari,
    keep Him hidden in your heart.
Lip should not touch lip,
no one should know.

राम नाम यों लीजिए, जाने सुमरन हार।
सहजो कै करतार ही, जाने ना संसार॥

बैठे लेटे चालते, खान पान व्यवहार।
जहां तहां सुमरण करो, सहजो हिये निहार॥

जागृत में सुमरण करो, सोवत में लौलाय।
सहजो इक रस ही रहे, तार टूट नहिं जाय॥

आठ पहर सुमरण करे, बिसरै ना क्षण एक।
अष्टादश अरु चार में, सहजो यही विशेष॥

सहजो सुमरण सब करें, सुमरण माहिं विवेक।
सुमरण कोई जानि है, कोटन मध्ये एक॥

Remember Ram in such a way
    that only you
    know what you do.
Sahajo says:
    The Master may know,
    the world should not.

Whether you are
    sitting, resting, walking,
    eating, drinking,
    or talking with others,
Here or there,
    Remembrance is easy,
    Sahajo says,
    when you look into your heart.

Remember Hari
    while you are awake.
Meditate on Him
    while you are asleep.
Sahajo says:
Let this one sentiment remain:
    the thread
    should never be broken.

Remember Him
    twenty-four hours a day.
Never forget Him
    for a single moment.
There are eighteen Puranas
and four Vedas,
Sahajo says,
and one special mantra.
Everyone remembers
    something.
Sahajo says:
    not everyone does it
    with discernment.
The one who remembers
    Hari
is one in a million.

जनम मरण बंधन कटें, टूटे यम की फांस।
राम नाम ले सहजिया, होय नहीं जग हांस॥

चौरासी के दुख छुटे, छप्पन नरक तिरास।
राम नाम ले सहजिया, यमपुर मिले न वास॥

गर्भ वास संकट मिटै, जठर अग्नि की आँच।
राम नाम ले सहजिया, मुख सों बोलो साँच॥

शील क्षमा संतोष, गह, पांचों इन्द्रिय जीत।
राम नाम ले सहजिया, मोक्ष होन की रीत॥

The ties of birth and death
are cut,
and Yama's noose
is broken,
when you invoke Ram's Name
Sahajiya.
The world
can never laugh at you.

You are freed from
the sorrows
of eighty-four lakh births,
and the fifty-six punishments
of hell,
when you invoke Ram's Name,
Sahajiya.
You will never live
in Yama's town.

You will never suffer
the misery of living in the womb,
or the heat
of the stomach's fires,
when you invoke Ram's Name,
Sahajiya.
May your mouth always speak
the truth.

You will be adorned
with virtue, mercy and peace,
you will conquer
the five senses.
when you invoke Ram's Name,
Sahajiya.
This is the way
to obtain liberation.

काम क्रोध मोह लोभ, मद तज भज हरिको नाम।
निश्चय सहजो मुक्ति हो, लहै अमर पुर धाम॥

74 ॥पंच विकार व भक्ति विरोध वर्णन॥

काम क्रोध मोह लोभ तन, ले सुमिरे हरि नाम।
मुक्ति न पावे सहजिया, ना रीझेंगे राम॥

कामी मति भिष्टल सदा, चलै चाल विपरीत।
शील नहीं सहजो कहै, नैनन माहिं अनीत॥

सदा रहे चितभंग ही, हिरदय थिरता नाहिं।
राम नाम के फल जिते, काम लहर बहि जाईं॥

You will abandon
lust, anger, attachment,
greed, passion,
when you chant Hari's Name.
I assure you,
Sahajiya,
you will be liberated,
and the immortal city
will be your home.

74 *A Description of the Five Faults which Create Opposition to Devotion*

If you chant Hari's Name
while your body is filled
with lust, anger, attachment,
greed and pride,
you will never be liberated,
Sahajiya,
and Ram will never be pleased.

A person of lustful inclinations
is always polluted.
His every act
is full of deceit.
He knows nothing of morality,
says Sahajo.
His eyes
are full of evil.

When the mind is always broken
and the heart is always active,
the waves of passion
will wash away
the benefits derived
from chanting Rama's Name.

सहजो क्रोधी अति बुरा, उल्टी समझे बात।
सब ही सूं ऐंठो रहै, करै वचन की घात॥

कूकर ज्यों भूंसत रहै, तामस मिले जु बोल।
घर बाहर दुख रूप है, बुधि रहे डाँवा डोल॥

मन मैला तन छीन हो, हरि सों लगै न नेह।
दुखी रहे सहजो कहे, मोह बसे जा देह॥

मोह मिरग काया वसै, कैसे उपजे खेत।
जो बोवै सोई चरै, लगेन हरि सों हेत॥

नीच लोभ जा घट बसै, झूँट कपट सों काम।
बोराया चहु दिशि फिरे, सहजो कारण दाम॥

Sahajo says:
    an angry person
    is always evil.
He understands everything
    the wrong way 'round.
He hates everyone he meets
    and kills them with his words.
He barks like a dog.
    His words are full of rage.
He spreads misery wherever he goes.
    His mind is never still.

He has no love
    to bind him to Hari.
He has a foul mind
    and a decayed body.
He lives in misery,
    says Sahajo,
because he is attached
    to nothing but himself.

When the deer of attachment
    lives in the body,
    no crop can grow in the field.
As soon as the seeds are sown,
    they are gone.
If only its love
    were attached to Hari!

When lowly greed
    lives in the body,
it makes friends
    with lies and deceit.
Distracted,
    it runs in all four directions.
Sahajo says:
    this is why
    he can never escape.

दृव्य हेत हरि कू भजे, धन ही की पर तीत।
स्वारथ ले सब सो मिले, अंतर की नहिं प्रीत॥

अभिमानी मुख धूर है, चहै बड़ाई आप।
डँभ लिये फूलो फिरे, करतो डरे न पाप॥

प्रभुताई को चाहत है, प्रभु को चाहे न कोय।
अभिमानी घट नीच है, सहजो ऊंच न होय॥

॥इति नाम महात्म्य का अंग संपूर्ण॥

He who worships Hari
for the sake of wealth,
has faith
only in money.
He who loves everyone he meets
only for what they can do for him.
has a heart
that is empty of love.

The face of the proud man
is covered with dust.
He longs to hear
other men praise him.
Swollen with pride,
he wanders about,
and has no fear of sin.

Everyone wants
to rule the world.
No one wants
to be ruled by God.
The proud man
is the lowest of the low.
Sahajo says:
he will never rise high.

Here End the Poems which Describe the Glory of the Name of the Lord

75 ॥लघुता का अंग वर्णन॥

॥दोहा॥

धन छोटा पन सुख महा, धिरग बड़ाई ख्वार।
सहजो नन्हा हूजिए, गुरु के वचन संसार॥

सहजो तारे सब सुखी, गहैं चंद अरु सूर।
साधु चाहे दीनता, चहै बड़ाई कूर॥

अभिमानी नाहर बड़ो, भरमत फिरे उजार।
सहजो नन्हीं वाकरी, प्यार करे संसार॥

सीस कान मुख नासिका, ऊंचे ऊँचे नाम।
सहजो लघुता कारने, सब कोई पूजे पांब॥

75 *A Description of Aspects of Humility*

Blessed is smallness,
        it brings much joy.
Accursed is greatness,
        which leads to ruin.
Sahajo says:
        be small.
Let the guru's words
        be your whole world.

Sahajo says:
        the stars are happy.
It is the sun and moon
        which suffer
        during an eclipse.
The sadhu
        seeks humility.
The wicked
        seek greatness.

The mighty lion
        wanders at will,
proudly seeking
        what it will kill.
Sahajo says:
        the nanny-goat is small
yet she is loved
        by one and all.

The head,
        ears, mouth and nose,
        are at the top of the body
        and are praised by all.
Sahajo says:
        the feet have no great beauty,
        yet it is they which are worshipped.

नन्नी चींटी भवन में, जहां तहां रस लेह।
सहजो कुंजर अति बड़ा, सिर में डारे खेह॥

सहजो दोयज चांद का, दर्श करे सब कोय।
नन्ने से दिन दिन बढ़े, अधकी चांदन होय॥

बड़ा भए आदर नहीं सहजो आंखिन देख।
कला सभी घट जायगी, कछू न रहसी शेष॥

सहजो नन्ना बालका, महल भूप के जांहि।
नारी परदा ना करें, गोद हि गोद खिलाहिं॥

बड़ा न जाने पाह हे, साहिब के दर बार।
द्वारे ही सूं लागि है, सहजो मोटी मार॥

वाले दीए चांदना, बड़ा दिये अंधियार।
सहजो तृण हलका तिरे, डूबे पत्थर भार॥

The tiny ant
    lives in a house
    and eats whatever it wants.
Sahajo says:
    the mighty elephant
    covers its head
    with dust.

Sahajo says:
    the new moon is auspicious,
    everyone views it with delight.
Day by day it increases
until
    it loses its beauty.
When the moon is full
    no one cares.
Sahajo says:
    you can see this yourself.
Day by day it wanes
until in the end
    nothing remains.

Sahajo says
    in the king's palace,
    the little boy can go
    wherever he wants.
The women will not cover themselves
    and he can sit on their lap.
The man has no access
    to the king in his court.
He must wait at the door,
and, says Sahajo,
is often beaten as well.

There is light with a small lamp,
    which dies when the flame gets too big.
Sahajo says:
    if you are like a blade of grass,
    you will float.
If you are heavy like a rock,
    you will drown.

भली गरीबी नम्रता, सके न कोई मार।
सहजो रुई कपास को, काटे ना तलवार॥

चरण दास सत गुरु कही, सहजो को यह चाल।
सके तो छोटा हूजिये, छूटे सब जंजाल॥

साहन को तो भय घना, सहजो निर्भय रँक।
कुँजर के पग बेडियां, चीटीं फिरे निशँक॥

ऊंचे उज्वल भाग से, आय मिले गुरुदेव।
प्रेम दिया नन्ना किया, पूरण पायो भेव॥

सहजो पूरण भाग सों, पाय लिये सुख दान।
नख सिख आई दीनता, भजे बड़ाई मान॥

सहजो पूरण भाग सो, पाये गुरु सुख दैन।
गए कुलक्षण देह से, लक्षण पायो चैन॥

Poverty and humility are good.
    No one will kill you
    to take them away.
Sahajo says:
    the sword cannot cut
    carded cotton.

Charandas, the true guru,
    shared this trick with Sahajo,
If you can, be small,
    then your life will be easy.

The rich live in fear.
Sahajo says:
    nothing bothers the poor.
The elephant's feet
    are bound with chains,
the ant wanders
    without a care.

Sahajo says:
By great good fortune,
    I met guru-deva.
He gave me his love
    and made me small.
No secrets were hidden from my eyes.

Sahajo says:
Purely by luck,
    I received the gift
    of Shukdeva's blessings.
Covered in humility,
    I sing his glory.

Sahajo says:
Purely by luck,
    I found the guru
    and received his blessings.
The evil marks were erased from my body,
and I was covered with good fortune.

औगण थे सो सब गए, राज करे उनतीस।
प्रेम झिला प्रीतम मिला, सहजो बारा शीश॥

76 ॥अथ प्रेम का अंग वर्णन॥

॥दोहा॥

चरण दास सत गुरु दिया, प्रेम पियाला छान।
सहजो मत वारी भई, तुरिया तत गलतान॥

प्रेम दिवाने जो भए, मन भयो चकना चूर।
छके रहें झूमत रहें, सहजो देख हजूर॥

प्रेम दिवाने जो भए, प्रीतम के रंग माहिं।
सहजो सुधि बुधि सब गई, तन की सोधी नाहिं॥

प्रेम दिवाने जो भए, कहें बहकते बैन।
कबहूं मुख हांसी छुटे, कबहूं बरसें नैन॥

प्रेम दिवाने जो भऐ, पलट गयो सब रूप।
सहजो दृष्टि न आवही, कहां रंक कहा भूप॥

प्रेम दिवाने जो भए, जाति वरण गहे छूट।
सहजो जग बौरा कहें, लोग गए सब फूट॥

All my defects left me,
the twenty-nine virtues rule my life.
I found love.
I found the beloved.
Sahajo bows her head
at his feet.

76 *The Beginning of the Description of Aspects of Love*

Charandas the true guru
prepared the cup of love for me.
Sahajo was intoxicated
and wallowed in the fourth stage.

The minds of those intoxicated with love
are smashed to smithereens.
Satisfied, they continue to sway,
Sahajo saw only the Master.

The minds of those intoxicated with love
are dyed the colour of the beloved.
Sahajo lost all consciousness
and was not aware of her body.

When the mind is intoxicated with love,
all speech is turned to babble.
Sometimes the mouth is filled with laughter,
sometimes the eyes are filled with tears.

When the mind is intoxicated with love,
the whole world is transformed.
Sahajo could no longer discriminate
between a pauper and a prince.

When the mind is intoxicated with love,
all concepts of caste and colour fall away.
The world called Sahajo mad,
people began to leave her.

प्रेम दिवाने जो भए, नेम धर्म गया खोय।
सहजो नर नारी हंसे, वा मन आनन्द होय॥

प्रेम दिवाने जो भए, सहजो डिग मिग देह।
पाँव पड़े कित के किती, हरि संभार जब लेह॥

कबहूं हक धक हो रहै, उठे प्रेम हित गाय।
सहजो आंख मुदी रहे, कबहूं सुधि हो जाय॥

मन में तो आनन्द है, तन बौरा सब अंग।
ना काहू के आसरे, ना काहू के संग॥

प्रेम लटक दुर्लभ महा, पावे गुरु के ध्यान।
अजपा सुमरण कहत हूं, उपजे केवल ज्ञान॥

॥इति प्रेम अंग संपूर्णम॥

When the mind is intoxicated with love,
        the rules of dharma disappear.
Men and women laughed at Sahajo,
        but her mind was filled with bliss.

When the mind is intoxicated with love,
        Sahajo's body sways.
The feet fall here, the feet fall there,
        but Hari always takes care of them.

Sometimes the heart beats loudly,
        sometimes it sings for the sake of love.
Sahajo was content to close her eyes,
        and was sometimes conscious, sometimes not.

When the mind is full of bliss,
        and the body is mad,
I am with no one,
        and no one is with me.

It is very hard to obtain love.
        Love comes only to those who
        meditate on the guru.
I will tell you how to chant
without chanting,
        true knowledge is born of love.

This Completes the Aspects of Love

77 ॥अथ अजपा गायत्री अंग वर्णन॥

ऐसा सुमरण कीजिए, सहज रहै लौलाय।
बिन जिह्वा बिन तालुवै, अंतर सुरति लगाय॥

हँसा सोहँ तार कर, सुरति मकरिया पोय।
उतरि उतरि फिर फिर चढ़े, सहजो सुमरण सोय॥

बरत बांध कर धरन में, कला गगन में खाय।
अधः उर्ध नटज्यों फिरै, सहजो राम रिझाय॥

लगै शून्य में टक टकी, आसन पद्म लगाय।
नाभि नासिका माहिं करि, सहजो रहे समाय॥

77 *Here Begin the Verses on the Unchanted Gayatri Mantra*

Remember God in such a way
that you remain in the simplicity
of deep meditation.
Shape ecstasy
in your innermost being,
without bringing the tongue
to the roof of the mouth.

The swan of the mantra "Soham", I am,
will carry your soul across the ocean
of existence.
Let ecstasy move
like a thread in a garland,
like a spider descending,
down, down, then up again.
Sahajo says:
chant in this way.

Having tied the chord of the breath to the earth,
let it leap high into the sky,
let it leap!
Bring it down, down,
like an acrobat.
Sahajo says:
this is the way to charm Ram.

With your eyes fixed ahead
and your legs firmly crossed,
dwell in nothingness.
Bring the naval
into the nose.
Sahajo says:
everything fits into place.

सहजो स्वांस तीरथ बहै, सहजो जो कोई न्हाय।
पाप पुन्य दोनों छुटें, हरि पद पहुचे जाय॥

हंकारे उठ नाभि सो, सँकारे हो लीन।
सहजो आजपा जाप है, चरणदास कह दीन॥

सब घट अजपा जाप है, हँसा सोहं पर्ब।
सुरत हिय ठहराये कर, सहजो बहु विधि निर्ब॥

सब घट व्यापक राम है, देही नाना भेक।
राव रंक चँडाल घट, सहजो दीपक एक॥

॥इति अजपा अंग संपूर्ण॥

In simplicity
    the breath flows
    like a holy river.
Sahajo says:
    whoever bathes there
washes away
    all sins and merits
and reaches Hari's feet.

The sound
ascends
from the naval,
gesturing
at extinction.
Sahajo,
this is the right way
to chant, Charandas told me.

Let your body chant
    the unchanted mantra,
while the swan of "soham"
    makes its measured way.
Having fixed ecstasy
    in your heart,
Sahajo says:
    study it carefully.

Each body is pervaded
    by Ram.
Each body wears many costumes:
    a lord and a pauper,
the lowest of the low.
Sahajo says:
    the one light burns
    in each vessel of clay.

Here End the Verses on the Unchanted

78 ॥अथ जगत मिथ्या का अंग वर्णन॥

॥दोहा॥

आतम में जागत नहीं, सुपने सोवत लोग।
सहजो सुपने होत है, रोग भोग अरु योग॥

कोट वर्ष इक क्षण लगे, ज्ञान दृष्टि जो होय।
विसर जगत इक अरु बने, सहजो सुपने सोय॥

ऐसे ही सब स्वप्न है, स्वर्ग मृत्यु पाताल।
तीन लोक छल रूप है, सहजो इन्दर जाल॥

अज्ञानी जाने नहीं, लिप्त भया करि भोग।
ज्ञानी तो दृष्टा भए, सहजो सुखी न शोक॥

मन माहीं वैराग्य है, ब्रह्म माहिं गलतान।
सहजो जगत अनित्य है, आतम नित्य पिछान॥

78 *Here Begins the Part Describing the Falseness of the World*

Those whose souls have not awakened,
are people of sleep and dreams.
Sahajo says:
    disease, pleasure and yoga
    are part of the dream.

A million years
    can seem like a moment,
when the vision of true knowledge
    happens to you.
By forgetting the world,
    one is transformed.
Sahajo says:
    that is the nature of the dream.

The nature of the dream
    creates all that we see:
    heaven, the mortal realm and hell.
The three worlds
    are built of lies.
Sahajo says:
    they are Indra's web.

The ignorant do not know this,
    they are too busy
    enjoying themselves.
Those who know
    become seers.
Sahajo says:
    they are neither happy
    nor sad.

Set detachment in the midst of your mind.
Live in the midst of Brahma.
Sahajo says:
    the world is temporary.
Recognise that
    the soul is eternal.

सहजो सुपने एक पल, बीते बरस पचास।
आँख खुली जब झूँठ है, ऐसे ही जग वास॥

मृग तृष्णा जल सांच है, जब लग निकट न जाय।
सहजो तब लग जग वन्यों, सत गुरु दृष्टि न पाय॥

जैसे बालक जल पिये, देख देख डर पाय।
समझ भई तब भ्रम लखा, सहजो रहा खिसाय॥

ज्ञानी को जग झूठ है, अज्ञानी को साँच।
कोट लाल कागज लिखे, सहजो बैठा वांच॥

जगत तरैया भोर की, सहजो ठहरत नाहिं।
जैसे मोती ओस का, पानी अँजुली माहिं॥

Sahajo says:
        during one moment in a dream
        fifty years may pass.
When you open your eyes
        you know you were deceived.
Thus is our stay in the world.

The water in a mirage is true,
        until you come close.
Sahajo says:
        the world remains
        until you see
        the sat-guru

Like a child swallowing water,
        he sees the pond,
        only the pond,
and is afraid.
As he grows older,
        he understands more
        and sees his mistake.
Sahajo says:
he will be embarrassed.

To one who knows,
        the world is false.
To the ignorant,
        it is true.
Like a heap of rubies
drawn on paper,
Sahajo says,
the wise must learn
to decipher what they see.

The world is like
        an army of stars
        in the dawn sky.
Sahajo says:
they will not stay.
Like a pearl made of dew,
like water in the hollow of your hands.

धूआ कांसा गढ़ बना, मनमें राज सजोय।
झांई मांई सहजिया, कबहूं साँच न होय॥

ऐसे ही जग झूँठ है, आत्म कूं थिर जान।
सहजो काल न खा सकै, ऐसो रूप पिछान॥

॥इति सत्य वैराग्य अंग संपूर्ण॥

The mind makes a fortress of smoke
and creates a glorious kingdom there.
It is a game of hide and seek, Sahajiya,
nothing happens. No truth is told.

Know that the world is false,
only the soul remains.
Sahajo says:
know the true self,
which time cannot destroy.

Here Ends Part 3 on Satya Vairagya

79 ॥अथ सच्चिदानंद का अंग वर्णन॥

॥दोहा॥

नया पुराना होय ना, घुन नहीं लागे जासु।
सहजो मारा ना मरे, भय नहिं व्यापै तासु॥

किरै घटै छीजै नहीं, ताहि न भिजवै नीर।
ना काहू के आसरे, ना काहू के सीर॥

रूप वरण जाके नहीं, सहजो रंग न देह।
मात पिता वाके नहीं, जाति पाँति नहिं गेह॥

सहजो उपजे ना मरै, सदवासी नहिं होय।
रात दिवस तामें नहीं, शीत उष्ण नहिं सोय॥

Part 4: ON SATCHIDANANDA AND OTHER MATTERS

79 *On Satchidananda: Truth, Knowledge and Bliss*

It is never new,
    never old,
the weevils cannot destroy it.
Sahajo says:
    you may kill it,
    but it will not die.
It has no fear.

Insects cannot eat it,
    it can never grow less.
It needs no one,
    it rules no one.

It has no form
    it has no caste.
Sahajo says,
    it has no colour,
    no body.
It has no mother,
    no father.
No caste, no creed,
    no home.

Sahajo says:
    it is not born,
    it does not die,
it has no home of its own.
It does not contain
    the day or the night.
It does not contain
    the heat or the cold.

आग जलाय सके नहीं, शस्त्र सके नहिं काट।
धूप सुखाय सके नहीं, पवन सके नहीं आट॥

मात पिता वाके नहीं, नहिं कुटुँब का साज।
सहजो वाहि न रंकता, ना काहू को राज॥

आदि अंत वाके नहीं, मध्य नहीं ता माहिं।
वार पार नहिं सहजिया, लघु दीरघ भी नाहिं॥

परलय में आवे नहीं, उतपति होय न फेर।
ब्रह्म अनादि सहजिया, घने हिराने हेर॥

जाके किरिया कर्म न, षट दरशन का भेष।
गुण अवगुण नहिं सहजिया, ऐसा पुरुष अलेख॥

रूप नाम गुण से रहित, पाँच तत्व से दूर।
चरणदास गुरु ने लखा, सहजो छिपा हजूर॥

Fire cannot burn it,
    swords cannot cut it.
The sun cannot scorch it,
    the wind cannot blow it away.

It has no parents,
    nor the fringe of a family.
Sahajo says:
    it knows neither poverty,
    nor the rich man's kingdom.

It has no beginning, no end,
    and no middle.
It has no limits,
    neither this side nor that.
O Sahajiya,
It is not big
    and it is not small.

It is not effected
    by the end of the world.
It is never reborn.
It is Brahma, without a beginning.
    O Sahajiya,
To search its depths
    is a terrible task.

It performs no rites,
    it wears none of the six philosophies.
It has no qualities, no defects,
    O Sahajiya,
Purusha, Supreme Spirit, is indescribable.

It has no form, no name, no qualities.
It has nothing to do with the five elements.
My guru Charandas has seen all this,
Sahajo sees nothing, may God forgive her.

आपा खोजे पाइए, और जतन नहिं कोय।
नीर क्षीर निरताय के, सहजो सुरत समोय॥

॥इति सच्चिदानन्द का अंग संपूर्ण॥

You will find yourself,
    when you lose yourself.
There is no other way.
The swan can tell
    what is milk, what is water.
Sahajo says:
    drown in passionate love of the Lord.

Here Ends Part 4 on Satchidananda

80 ॥अथ नित्य अनित्य सांख्य मत वर्णन॥

॥दोहा॥

भिन्न भिन्न दोनों करे, वही सांख्य मत भेद।
जीवन और विदेह सो, मुक्ति पाय तज खेद॥

जाग्रत और शुषोपति, स्वप्न अवस्था तीन।
काया ही से होत है, घटै बढ़ै होय क्षीन॥

तुरिया इक रस आतमा, इन से परे निहार।
इन्द्री मन गह ना सके, सहजो तत्व अपार॥

जिह्वा चाख सके नहीं, श्रवण सुने नहिं ताहि।
नैन विलोक सके नहीं, नासा त्वचा न पाय॥

अनुभय ही सूँ जानिये, चित बुधि थक थक जाहि।
तीन भाँति अहंकार का, सोभी पावे नाहि॥

Part 5: ON KNOWLEDGE AND DEVOTION

80 *Here Begins a Description of the Temporal and Eternal Aspects of Sankhya Doctrine*

Purusha and Prakriti are different,
    yet they are one.
This is the secret teaching
    of Sankhya doctrine.
Turn away from confusion
    and find liberation
beyond the body, as Janaka taught.

Awake, asleep and dreaming,
these are the three stages of life.
Together they shape the body,
as it decreases, increases and decays.
The soul should look beyond these
to the fourth stage,
which the mind and senses cannot understand.
Sahajo says:
its nature is limitless.

The tongue cannot taste it.
    The ears cannot hear it.
The eye cannot see it.
    The nose cannot smell it.
The skin cannot touch it.

You can only know it from experience.
    The mind grows weary
    trying to understand it.
There are three types of pride:
    none of them ever finds it.

जाके रस अरु रूप ना, गंध नहीं वा ठौर।
शब्द नहीं सपरस नहीं, सहजो वह कछु और॥

गुण तीनों से है परे, तामें रूप न रेख।
बोध रूप सहजो कहै, ब्रह्म दृष्टि कर देख॥

81 ॥अथ निर्गुण सगुण संशय निवारण भक्ति अंग वर्णन॥

॥दोहा॥

निराकार आकार सब, निरगुण अरु गुणवंत।
है नाहीं सूं रहित है, सहजो वह भगवंत॥

नाम नहीं अरु नाम सब, रूप नहीं सब रूप।
सहजो सब कुछ ब्रह्म है, हरि परगट हरि गूप॥

कहा कहूं कहा कहि सकूं, अचरज अलख अभेव।
सुने अचंभा सा लगे, सहजो ब्रह्म अलेव॥

It has no essence and no form,
no smell, no location.
It cannot be described.
It cannot be touched.
Sahajo says:
It is different
from all that we know.

It is beyond the three gunas.
It has no form and no shape.
You will only see it, says Sahajo,
when you look with Brahma's eyes.

81 *Here Begins the Description of the Role of Bhakti in Removing Doubts about God-with-Form and God-beyond-Form*

It has no form and all forms,
no form and all attributes.
It has no being
and is complete in every way.
Sahajo says:
It is the Lord.

It has no name and every name,
no form and every form.
Sahajo says:
everything is Brahma.
Hari revealed.
Hari concealed.

What may I tell?
What can I say?
It is inexpressible,
indivisible, unlimited.
I am wonderstruck
when I hear about Brahma.
Sahajo says:
It is holy.

वही आप परगट भया, ईश्वर लीला धार।
माहिं अयोध्या और वृज, कोतक किए अपार॥

चार बीस अवतार धर, जन की करी सहाय।
राम कृष्ण पूरण भए, महिमा कही न जाय॥

भक्त हेत हरि आइया, पृथ्वी भार उतार।
साधुन की रक्षा करी, पापी डारे मार॥

निर्गुण से सर्गुण भयो, संत उधारन हार।
सहजो की डंडोत हैं, ताकूँ बारँबार॥

जाके रूप अनँत है, जाके नाम अनेक।
ताके कौतुक बहुत हैं, सहजो नाना भेख॥

गीता में श्री कृष्ण ने, बचन कहे दो खोल।
सब जीवन में मैं वसूँ, के चर कहा अडोल॥

This one
        manifests itself!
Ishwara plays many parts.
In Ayodhya and Braj,
God played His many games.

Dressed in the guise
        of twenty-four avatars,
God comes to protect His people.
Rama and Krishna
        were complete incarnations.
How can I tell of His glory?

For the sake of His devotees,
        Hari comes
to free the earth of its burden.
He protected the good,
he killed the evil.

From God-beyond-Form,
        He became God-with-Form,
to deliver the saints.
Sahajo bows before Him
        again and again.

He, whose form is infinite
        and has many names,
plays many games.
        Sahajo says:
He wears many disguises.

In the Gita, Shri Krishna spoke
        of the two modes
        in which He reveals Himself.
"All life resides in me:
  the animate
  and the inanimate."

मैं अखँड व्यापक सकल, सहज रहा भर पूर।
ज्ञानी पावे निकट ही, मूरख जाने दूर॥

योगी पावे योग से, ज्ञानी लहै विचार।
सहजो पायो भक्ति सूं, जाके प्रेम अधार॥

धन्य यशोदा नंद धन, धन वृज मँडल देश।
आदि निरँजन सहजिया, भयो ग्वाल के बेश॥

82 ॥चौपाई॥

नेति नेति कहि वेद पुकारे,
सो अधरन पर मुरली धारे।
जाकूं ब्रह्मादिक मुनि ध्यावें,
ताहि पूत कहि नंद वुलावे॥

शिव सनकादिक अन्त न पावै,
सो सखियन संग रास रचावै।
संयम साधन ध्यान न आवें,
सो ग्वालन संग खेल मचावे॥

अनंत लोक मेटे उपजावै,
सो मोहन वृज राज कहावै।
निराकार निर्भय निर्वाणा,
कारण संत धरे तन नाना॥

"I am indivisible
and all-pervasive."
Sahajo says:
He never changes.
"The wise find me close at hand.
The fool believes that I am far away."
"The yogi finds me through yoga.
The wise finds me through the mind."
Sahajo says:
I found Him through devotion.
I found Him through love.

Blessed is Yashoda
blessed is Nanda,
blessed is the land of Braj.
Niranjan, primal pure Being,
took the guise of a cowherd,
Sahajiya.

82

He, whom the Vedas describe
as "Not this" and "Not that",
placed the flute on His lips.
He upon whom
Brahma and the learned
meditate,
Nanda called "Son".

He whose end
Shiva and the four sons of Brahma
could not find,
danced in the company of the cowherd girls.
He, who cannot be found
through asceticism or meditation,
played games with the cowherd boys.
He, who creates and destroys
many worlds,
is Mohan, the charmer, king of Braj.
He, who is formless, fearless,
eternal bliss,
assumed many forms
for the sake of the saints.

निर्गुण सर्गुन भेद न दोई,
आदि अंत मध एक हि होई।
गूंगे के सपने सम बाता,
सहजो करे कौन के साथा॥

83 ॥दोहा॥

निर्गुण सर्गुण एक प्रभु, देखा समझ विचार।
सत गुरु ने आखें दई, निश्चय किया निहार॥

सहजो हरि बहु रँग हैं, वही प्रकट वही गूप।
जल पाले में भेद ना, ज्यो सूरज अरु धूप॥

चरणदास गुरु की दया, गया सकल सँदेह।
छूटे बाद जिवाद सब, भई सहज गत लेह॥

गुरु बिन मारग ना मिले, गुरु बिन लहे न ज्ञान।
गुरु बिन सहजो धुँध है, गुरु बिन पूरी हान॥

सतगुरु बिन भटकत फिरे, परसत पाथर नीर।
सहजो कैसे मिट सके, यम जालिम की पीर॥

God-with-Form and God-beyond-Form
are not two, are not different.
His beginning, middle and end
are one, they are the same.
It is like the dream of a mute,
how can he describe what he has seen?

83

God-with-Form and God-beyond-Form are one God.
I have thought about this and seen it for myself.
The true guru gave me eyes. It is certain.
I know because I have seen it for myself.

Sahajo says:
Hari has many colours.
He is manifest and He is hidden.
There is no difference between water and ice.
There is no difference between the sun and its light.

By the mercy of Charandas, my guru,
        my doubts were erased,
I was freed from logic and debate.
He made me "Sahajo".
He established me in simplicity.

Without the guru,
        you will never find your way.
Without the guru,
        you will never know anything.
Without the guru,
        you will live in darkness.
Without the guru,
        you will lose everything.

Without the true guru,
        you will wander forever,
meditating on idols of stone
        and rivers of water.
Sahajo says:
        How can these things
remove Yama's cruel pains?

पूजे नवगृह देवता, पित्तर सती अकूत।
सहजो कैसे सुलझ है, हो रहा सूत कुसूत॥

गुरु कू जानत है नहिं, वनिता सुत के मोह।
साधुन की निन्दा करें, हरि सो राखें द्रोह॥

अनन्य भक्ति उपजी नहीं, गुरु सो नाहीं सीर।
सहजो मिले न सिन्धु से, ज्यों तलाव को नीर॥

जनक विदेही परम गुरु, दादा गुरु शुकदेव।
सहजो की दंडवत है, चरणदास गुरु लेव॥

84 ॥छप्पय॥

हरि प्रसाद की सुता नाम है सहजो बाई,
दूसर कुल में जन्म सदा गुरु चरण सहाई॥

चरणदास गुरु भेद मोहि अगम बतायो,
योग युक्ति सो दुर्लभ सुलभ कर दिखरायो॥

सब साधुन परणाम करि कर जोरू सिर नाय कै,
यही दान मोहि दीजिये भक्ति करूँ चितलाय कै॥

॥इति सहजोबाई कृत सहज प्रकाश समाप्तम॥

You will worship the nine planets,
Parvati, the gods
and innumerable ancestors,
Sahajo says:
When the thread is tangled,
how can it be made straight?

If you don't know the guru,
you will be attached to your wife and son.
You will slander the saints
and be hostile to Hari.

If you do not bow before the guru,
devotion will never be born in your heart.
Sahajo says: you will be like a drop of water
caught in a lake,
which never finds the ocean.

Great grandfather Videha was the supreme teacher.
Shukdev initiated my Master.
Sahajo's prostrations to you, Charandas, my guru,
accept my homage.

84

I am Hari Prasad's daughter,
my name is Sahajo Bai.
I was born in a Dhusar family
and depend forever on Charandas.

Charandas my guru told me
the secret of the Inaccessible:
Through the discipline of yoga,
what is hard to obtain
becomes easy to find.
He showed me this.

Having bowed before the holy ones,
hands together, head held low,
I ask for this one gift,
may my mind be filled with devotion.

Here ends the Sahaj Prakash, written by Sahajo Bai

85 ॥दोहा॥

फागुन महिना अष्टमी शुल्कपक्ष बुधवार।
संवत अठ्ठारैसै हुता सहजो किया विचार॥

गुरु स्तुतिके करन को उपज्यों हिए हुलांस।
होते होते हो गई पोथी सहज प्रकाश॥

दिल्ली शहर सुहावना परिक्षत पुर में वास।
तहां समापत ही हुई नौका सहज प्रकाश॥

सहज प्रकाश पोथी कही चरणदास परताप।
पढ़े सुने जो प्रीति सों भागै सब ही पाप॥

85

On the eighth day of the lunar fortnight,
a Wednesday, in the light half of the month,
the month of Phalgun, the year 1800 Samvat[1],
Sahajo was overcome with joy.

The joy, born in her heart,
arose from her desire to praise her guru,
and gradually formed this small book,
Sahaj Prakash, The Light of Simplicity.

While residing in Pariksit Pura,
in the pleasant city of Delhi,
She finished the boat of *Sahaj Prakash*.

Sahaj Prakash is a small book,
inspired by the greatness of Charandas.
Whoever reads or hears it with love,
will never be troubled by sin.

1 1743 C.

1 ॥दोहा॥

परणम श्री शुकदेव कू जिन पर वारूं प्राण।
सोलह तिथि वर्णन करू जिनका दीजे ज्ञान॥

चरण दास के चरणको निस दिन राखूँ ध्यान।
ज्ञान भक्ति अरु योग की तिथि मैं करूँ बखान॥

2 ॥कुंडलियां ३०॥

॥मावस॥

मावस मम्मा रर्रा दो अंक को राखो हिरदय माहिं,
धर्मराज जांचै नहीं लेखा मांगे नाहिं।
लेखा मांगे नाहि जाय नहि यमपुर बांधा,
ऐसे निर्मल नाम को, विसरे सो आंधा।
टीका चारों वेद का महिमा कही न जाय,
अवसर बीत्यो जात है सहजो सुमिर अघाय॥

PART 6: POEMS ON DAYS AND NUMBERS

1

I bow to Shri Shukdev,
to whom I sacrifice my life.
I will now describe the sixteen days of the lunar fortnight,
may he teach me what I should know.

I bow at the feet of Charandas,
and remember him each day and night
I now will describe the days
and relate them to knowledge,
devotion and yoga.

2 *Kundaliya Stanzas on the Phases of the Moon*

The New Moon

At the beginning of the lunar fortnight,
keep the two letters, Ma and Ra, in your heart.
Although Dharmaraja, the Lord of Death, accepts
everyone else,
he will set you no tests and ask for no explanations.
He will ask for no explanations
and not force you to go to Yamapur in chains.
Those who forget the Name of Rama are blind.
The commentaries of the four Vedas cannot describe it.
Even now this opportunity is slipping away.
Sahajo says: be filled with God's name.

॥एकम ॥

पड़वा पानी कासा बुलबुला यह तन ऐसा होय,
पीय मिलन की ठानिए रहिए ना पड़ सोय।
रहिए ना पड़ सोय बहुरि नहि मनुषा देही,
आपन ही कूं खोज मिलै जब राम सनेही।
हरि को भूले जो फिरें सहजो जीवन छार,
सुखिया जब ही होयगा सुमिरेगा करतार॥

॥दोयज ॥

दोयज धंधा जगत का लाग रहा दिन रैन,
कुटुंब महा दुख देत है कैसे पावे चैन।
कैसे पावे चैन बिना साधौं की संगत,
दुनिया रंग पतंग मजीठी गुरु की रंगत।
जनम मरण तासों छुटैं सहजो दरसे राम,
चौरासी के दुख मिटें पावे निजपुर धाम॥

One

On the first day of the lunar fortnight,
    remember that the body is like a bubble of water.
Be determined to meet the Beloved,
    do not remain in your bed.
Do not remain in your bed,
    it is not easy to gain a human birth.
When you search within yourself,
    you will find Ram's love.
Those who forget Hari wander in darkness.
    Sahajo says: their lives are dust.
You will only be happy
    when you chant the Name of the Creator.

Two

On the second day of the lunar fortnight,
    remember that the trade of the world goes on continually.
The family causes great sorrow,
    how can you ever find rest?
How can you ever find rest,
    if you do not keep the company of the good and the holy?
The world fades like the colours on a kite,
    only the dark red of the guru's dye remains.
It removes the stains of birth and death.
    Sahajo says: when you see Ram,
the eighty-four lakh sorrows will be erased
and you will find your true home in His city.

॥तीज॥

तीज तनिक सुख कारने बहुत फंसाए जीव,
लालच लागे यों फिरैं जैसे माखी घीव।
जैसे माखी घीव डूब कर निकसै नाही,
ऐसे यह नर डूब रहा कुनबे के माही।
मानुष देही पाय कर सहजो डारी खोय,
यमपुर बांधे वे चले चौरासी दुख होय॥

॥चतुर्थी॥

चौथ चहूं दिशि तिमिर है महा घोर भय मान,
मूरख नर सोवत तहां मिथ्या जग सच जान।
मिथ्या जग सच जान सत्य कूं जानत नाही,
बन बन ढूंढ़त फिरे राम अपने ही माही।
ज्यों मेंहदी में रंग है लकड़ी मध्य हुतास,
सहजो काया खोज ले काहे रहत उदास॥

Three

On the third day of the lunar fortnight,
    remember that many have become ensnared
    for the sake of brief pleasures.
Driven by greed they gather
    like a fly drawn to ghee.
Like the fly drawn to ghee,
    they drown, they cannot escape.
In the same way,
    many drown in the midst of their families.
Having found a human birth,
    Sahajo says: they waste it.
They set off for Yama's city in chains,
    and the eighty-four lakh sorrows happen again.

Four

On the fourth day of the lunar fortnight,
    remember that darkness lies all around you
    and makes all men afraid.
Fools sleep in darkness,
    believing the false world to be true.
Believing the false world to be true,
    they do not know the truth.
They search for Ram in the forest,
    and He lives within their heart,
like the red in henna,
and the sacrificial fire in a piece of wood.
Sahajo says:
    search within your body.
    Why be sad?

॥पंचमी॥

पांचों इन्द्री वश करो मन जीतन की ठान,
पवन रोक अनहद लगे पावो पद निर्वाण।
पावो पद निर्वाण करो तुम ऐसी करनी,
आसन, संयम, साध, बंध लागे जब धरनी।
चित, बुध, अहंकार, को करो इकट्ठे आन,
सहजो थिर मन होय जब निश्चय लागै ध्यान॥

॥षष्टी॥

छट छहों कमल को छेदकर सतवे में घर छाव,
रसना उलट लगाय कर जब आगे कूं धाव।
जब आगे को धाव देखकर जगमग ज्योती,
बिन दामिनि चमकार सीप बिन उपजे मोती।
हंस हंस जहां होत हैं ओं ओं नित होय,
चरणदास यों कहत हैं सहजो सुरत समोय॥

Five

Conquer the five senses.
    Resolve to conquer your mind.
Stop your breath. Listen to the unstruck sound,
    and you will find spiritual perfection.
You will find spiritual perfection
    if you do these things:
practice yoga postures, self-restraint,
    and regular spiritual disciplines.
    Learn to apply the inner psychic locks.
Unite your mind, intellect and sense of self.
Sahajo says:
    when your mind is stable,
    meditation will be easy.

Six

On the sixth day of the lunar fortnight,
    having pierced the six lotuses,
    rest in the seventh chakra.
Bring the tip of your tongue
    into the back of your mouth;
    this will deepen your meditation.
This will deepen your meditation
    and you will see a dazzling light.
The sky will shine
    without lightning.
A gleaming pearl will form
    without any shell.
The soul, the swan will come to feed,
when the saints chant "Om",
    each day "Om..."
Charandas told me:
    Sahajo,
    let yourself sink
    into ecstasy.

॥सप्तमी ॥

सातें सत संगत ही कीजिए सत ही कथिए ज्ञान,
सत ही मुख से बोलिए सत ही कीजे ध्यान।
सत ही कीजे ध्यान हद्द तज बेहद लागो,
तीन अवस्था छोड़ जाय तुरिया में पागो।
निराकार निर्गुण तहाँ इक रस चेतन रूप,
रात दिना सहजो नहीं नहीं छाँव अरु धूप॥

॥अष्टमी ॥

आठौं आठन कूं जाने नहीं दस को नाही भेद,
चौबीसौ समझे नहीं कैसे छूटे खेद।
कैसे छूटे खेद पंच को जीते नाही,
और पचीसों संग रहें उनही के माही।
दोय सदा लागी रहें चौरासी के फेर,
चरणदास यों कहत हैं सहजो आपा हेर॥

Seven

On the seventh day of the lunar fortnight,
    keep the company of those who are holy,
    who speak of what they know, who speak the truth.
Speak the truth. Meditate on the truth.
Meditate on the truth. Let it take you
    beyond all limits
    to the limitless.
Abandoning the three stages
    of wakefulness, sleep and dream,
    immerse yourself in the fourth.
There you will find God-without-Form.
    God-beyond-all-forms,
    the one living consciousness,
    one true essence.
There you will find no night or day,
    Sahajo,
no light and no shadow.

Eight

On the eight day of the lunar fortnight,
    remember the eight deadly sins
    which many forget,
the secret of the ten organs of cognition and action,
and the twenty-four elements of nature,
    which they do not understand either.
    How can they be free of suffering?
How can they be free of suffering,
    when they have not conquered the five senses,
    when the twenty-five remain,
    hidden there?
Those who are attached to duality
    will live in the circuit of eighty-four lakh births.
Charandas told me:
    Sahajo,
    abandon the ego.

॥नवमी॥

नवमी निन्दा हिंसा त्यागकर तापस कूं दे पीठ,
चित को स्थिर कीजिए नासा आगे दीठ।
नासा आगे दीठ जहां कछु देखो भाई,
पांच तत्व दरसाय और अचरज दरसाई।
तिर देवा अरु आट सिधि देखो इन्दर भूप,
चरणदास यों कहत है साधन आधिक अनूप॥

॥दशमी॥

दशमी दसों दिशा भरपूर है ता में ये सब पिंड,
ज्यों सरवर में बुलबुला ब्रह्म बीच ब्रह्मण्ड।
ब्रह्म बीच ब्रह्मंड तास को वार न पारा,
ऐसा तत्व अगाध नेति कह निगम पुकारा।
चरण दास कहै सहजिया गुरु सो लेवो ज्ञान,
नैना होहि अनंद ही जब यह पावे ध्यान॥

Nine

On the ninth day of the lunar fortnight,
    abandon slander and violence,
    renounce harsh asceticism.
Make your mind stable. Focus on the tip of your nose.
Focus on the tip of your nose, where you will see many things,
    my brother.
You will see the five elements, many miracles,
the three gods, the eight siddhis, and Lord Indra.
Charandas told me:
    these are rare accomplishments.

Ten

On the tenth day of the lunar fortnight,
    when all ten directions are full of light,
    the body dwells in the midst of that light.
It is like a bubble in the ocean.
    Like the egg of Brahma
    in the vastness of Brahma's body.
Like the egg of Brahma in the vastness of Brahma's body,
    with no limits, this side or that.
It is unfathomable. The Vedic texts call it
    "not this" and "not that".
Charandas told me:
    Sahajiya,
    when you receive true knowledge from the guru,
    your eyes will be filled with bliss
    each time you meditate.

॥एकादशी ॥

ग्यार संगति जो चहत हो तजो जगतकी आस,
कलह कल्पना छोड़ कर आतम में कर बास।
आतम में कर बास खेच इन्द्री दस लाओ,
मन स्थिर जबहोय सुरत अरु निरत मिलाओ।
ध्याता लागे ध्यान में ध्यान देह के मांहि,
जन्म मरण मिट सहजिया उपजै बिनसै नांहि॥

॥द्वादशी ॥

द्वादश दावा दूर करि दावे में ही दुःख,
राग, द्वेष अरु आपदा अकस निवारे सुख।
अकस निवारे सुख मोहि चरण दास दुहाई,
तामस मन से त्याग तास में बहुत भलाई।
काम, क्रोध, मोह लोभ कूं ज्ञान अग्नि में जार,
मन निर्मल हो सहजिया आनंद लहै अपार॥

Eleven

On the eleventh day of the lunar fortnight,
    if you desire to keep company with the true,
    you must give up all hope in the world,
Stop your quarrels. Leave off regret. Withdraw into yourself.
Withdraw into yourself. Bring all your senses inside yourself.
When the mind is stable,
    the embodied soul and the Absolute
    will be as one.
The meditator becomes the meditation.
The body becomes the act of meditation.
Birth and death are erased,
    Sahajiya,
    you will not be born,
    you will not die.

Twelve

On the twelfth day of the lunar fortnight,
    claim nothing as your own.
    Desire leads to sorrow.
Abandon attachment, hatred, ambition and love
    and you will be happy.
Abandon love and you will be happy. I swear this,
    Charandas told me so.
Renounce the darkness of your mind,
    and great good will follow.
Burn lust, anger and attachment
    in the fire of knowledge.
Let your mind be pure,
    Sahajiya,
    and you will experience
    unbounded bliss.

॥त्रयोदशी॥

तेरस तन अचरज महा क्षण भंगी छल रूप,
देखत ही देखत गए कहा रंक कहा भूप।
कहा रंक कहा भूप कोई रहने नहिं पावै,
इत सो सब ही जांय, बहुरि उतसों नहि आवें।
यह जानत हू घर रचै महल द्रव्य संतान,
हांसी आवे सहजिया ए मूरख मस्तान॥

॥चर्तुदशी॥

चौदस चौरासी भुगती घनी बहुत सही यममार,
भरम फिरे तिंहु लोक में तऊ न मानी हार।
तऊ न मानी हार मुक्ति की चाह न नीकी,
हीरा देहीं पाय मोल माटी के दीनी।
मूरख नर समझे नहीं समझाया बहु बार,
चरणदास कहैं सहजिया सुमरे ना करतार॥

Thirteen

On the thirteenth day of the lunar fortnight,
the body is a mystery,
it can be destroyed in a moment,
it is filled with deceit.
You can die in the blink of an eye,
whether you be a prince or a pauper.
Whether you be a prince or a pauper, no one lives forever.
We all depart. No one returns.
We know this, but we take up residence
in a palace, our money, or our children.
Sahajiya laughs:
what stupid, conceited fools you all are.

Fourteen

On the fourteenth day of the lunar fortnight,
you have endured eighty-four lakh births,
you have been beaten many times by Yama,
you have wandered confused through the three worlds,
and still you do not accept your defeat.
You do not accept your defeat, you don't want to be liberated.
You have found the precious jewel of a human birth,
and given it away dirt-cheap.
You fool, why won't you understand,
when you have heard the truth so many times before?
Charandas told me:
Sahajiya,
they have forgotten the Creator.

॥पूर्णिमा॥

पूनो पूरा गुरु मिले मेटे सब संदेह,
सोवत सूं चैतन्य हो देखे जागृत गेह।
देखे जागृत गेह जहां से सुपना आया,
जग कूं जाना साँच रूप अपना बिसराया।
चरण दास कहैं सहजिया गुरु चरणन चित लाव,
तिमिर मिटे अज्ञान का ज्ञान चांदना पाव॥

3 ॥दोहा॥

सोलह तिथि पूरण भई सहजो करी बखान।
चरण दास की दया सूं मिटें सकल अज्ञान॥

पढ़े, लिखे, सुन प्रीति सों ताके पाप नसाहिं।
अरु ऐसी करनी करै मुक्ति रूप हो जाहिं॥

॥इति सोलह तिथि संपूर्ण॥

The Full Moon

On the day of the full moon,
    find the Perfect Master,
    he will erase all your doubts.
Be conscious, even when you are asleep.
    When you are awake, know your true home.
Know your true home and how the body builds dreams.
If you believe the world to be true,
    you will forget who you are.
Charandas told me:
    Sahajiya,
    if you lay your mind at the guru's feet
    the moonlight of knowledge
    will dispel the darkness of ignorance.

3

Sahajo has described
    the sixteen facets of the lunar fortnight.
By the grace of Charandas,
    all ignorance is erased.
Whoever reads, writes or hears my words
    with love,
    will be freed from sin.
And every deed they do
    will be the act of a liberated soul.

Here End the Sixteen Days

॥अथ सात वार वर्णन॥

1 ॥दोहा॥

नमो नमो शुक देव जी, तुमरी शरण गही।
मेरे सिरपर कर धरो, चरणों लाग रही॥

सात वार वर्णन करूं, कुँडलि मांहि उचार।
अपने मुख सो कहत हूं, तुम को हिरदय धार॥

2 ॥कुंडलिया॥

॥मंगलवार॥

मंगल माली राम है जाका यह जग बाग,
निसि दिन ताही से रहे वाही सेती लाग॥
वाही सेती लाग करी जिन यह गुलजारी,
पात पात की खबर डाल सब लागें प्यारी।
आपन हूं कूं मान ले उसी डाल का फूल,
चरण दास कहै सहजिया ऐसे समझो कूल॥

Here Begins the Description of the Seven Days of the Week

1

Again and again, I bow before Shukdev ji,
and take refuge in you.
Place your hand on my head,
give me your blessing.
I shall not leave your feet.
I will now describe the seven days of the week,
in kundaliya stanzas.
The words I speak are mine,
the love I have is yours,
you live in my heart.

2 *Kundaliya Stanzas*

Tuesday

On Tuesday, Ram is the gardener,
the whole garden is his.
May I stay with him, night and day,
may I never leave his side,
May I never leave his side,
he makes the garden grow.
He knows every leaf
and cares for every branch.
Be a flower on a branch
in his garden.
Charandas said:
Sahajiya,
be a flower in his garden.

॥बुधवार॥

बुध वाडी में फल घने जो पै देवै वाड़,
रखवाली के बिन किए पांचों करें उजाड़।
पाचों करें उजाड़ पचीसों चर चर जाई,
सावधान जो होय सुई वाके फल खाई।
चरण दास कहें सहजिया ऐसे समझ बिचार,
तेरी काया में खिले भांति भाँति गुलजार॥

॥गुरुवार॥

वृहस्पति वारी आइया पाई मनुषा देह,
सो तन क्षण क्षण घटत है भयो जात है खेह।
भयो जात है खेह बहुरि लाहा कब लै हो,
बेगहि समझ संभार नहीं बहुतै पछितै हो।
आगा पिछा क्या करे सकल वासना त्याग,
चरणदास कहै सहजिया हरि सुमरन सूं लाग॥

Wednesday

On Wednesday, the trees around the garden
are heavy with fruit.
If you are not careful, five savage beasts
can destroy your garden.
Five can destroy your garden,
they can eat the twenty-five,
eat the elements.
If you are aware
the fruits will be yours.
Charandas said:
Sahajiya,
your thoughts are like flowers
which blossom in your body.

Thursday

On Thursday, you entered the garden
when you obtained a human birth.
The body diminishes
and turns to dust.
It turns dust,
don't let this opportunity pass.
Understand this, take care,
otherwise you will be filled with regret.
Why do you run to and fro?
Abandon your passions at once.
Charandas said:
Sahajiya,
devote yourself to the worship of Hari.

॥शुक्रवार॥

शुक्कर सर उपदेश का लगा कलेजे मांहि,
ते नर पशू समान हैं या दुनिया के मांहि।
या दुनिया के मांहि सदा चक्कर में डोलें,
जनम मरण दुख महा तास की गांठ न खोलें।
ऐसे मूरख बावरे भोंदू मूढ गंवार,
चरणदास कहैं सहजिया भरमे बारंबार॥

॥शनिवार॥

थावर थिर करतार है और सकल मिट जाय,
जाते सूं मत प्रीत कर रहते चित्त लगाय।
रहते चित्त लगाय तासु ने जग उपजावा,
वाकी शरणैं जाहु करै बहु विधि सों छाया।
ऐसा हरि का नाम है जनम मरण मिट जाय,
चरणदास कहै सहजिया सांचे सूं मन लाय॥

Friday

On Friday, the arrows of the guru's words
    pierced my heart.
Some men live in the world like animals.
They live like animals and stagger in circles.
Birth and death bring great sorrow,
    they are like large knots.
Such men are fools, madmen,
    simpletons and boors.
Charandas said:
    Sahajiya,
    they are deceived
    again and again.

Saturday

The Creator is eternal and unchanging,
    everything else will pass away.
Do not love that which comes and goes,
    think of that which is permanent.
Think of that which is permanent,
    it created the world.
Take refuge in that which can protect you
    in every way.
Take refuge in Hari's name
    which can put an end
    to birth and death.
Charandas said:
    Sahajiya,
    think on the truth.

॥रविवार॥

ऐत जु आए जगत में हरि सुमरण के काज,
ह्यां कुछ कीया और ही नैक न आई लाज।
नैक न आई लाज काज सब खोटे कीन्हे,
सदा रहा अज्ञान राम घट में नहि चीन्हे।
जै हो जन्म गंवाय कर पछतावा रहि जाय,
चरणदास कहैं सहजिया कहा कियो तन पाय॥

॥सोमवार॥

सोम श्रीपति सेइए गुरु का आयुस लेहु,
संगत अरु हरि कथा ताही में चित्त देहु।
ताही में चित देहु और ऊँचा न या पातें,
सकल धर्म हरि बिना जगत की मिथ्या बातें।
चरणदास कहैं सहजिया भक्ति शिरोमणि जान,
तन, मन, चित, बुध प्राण कूंतामे दीजे आन॥

Sunday

On Sunday, you were born into the world,
to chant Hari's name.
You did something else and were not ashamed.
You were not ashamed that all your deeds were false.
You remained in ignorance
and did not recognise Ram.
Well done! You have wasted your life
and have only regrets.
Charandas said:
Sahajiya, what did you do
with the body
you were given?

Monday

On Monday, worship Vishnu,
with your guru's permission.
Keep good company and hear stories of Hari.
Hear stories of Hari, nothing else matters.
Without Hari, all religions are worldly and false.
Charandas said:
Sahajiya,
nothing is greater than devotion.
Give your body, mind, thoughts,
intellect and life,
to the Lord.

3 ॥दोहा॥

सात वार यह मैं कहे तामें हरि का भेद।
जो कोई समझे प्रीति सों छूटे सब की खेद॥

सातों वारों बीच में जग उपजै मर जाय।
सहजो बाई हरि जपो आवा गबन न साय॥

॥इति शब्द सप्तवार संपूर्ण॥

3

I have described
    the seven days of the week,
each filled with the secret of Hari
Whoever understands my words
    with love
    will have no regrets.
In this world
    we are born each day
    and we die
    on one of the seven days of the week.
Sahajo Bai says:
    chant Hari's name,
    and you will destroy
    the cycle of birth and death.

Here End the Seven Days of the Week

॥अथ शब्द वर्णन॥

1 ॥राग गौरी॥

नमो नमो गुरु तुम शरणा

तुमरे ध्यान भरम भय भागे जीते पाचौ और मना
दुख दारिद्र मिटे तब किरपा कर्म कटै जो होय घना
लोक और परलोक जु सुधरे पगलागे होय ज्ञान गुना
चरण छुए सब गति मति पजटै पारस जैसे लागे सुना
सीप परस स्वाती भयो सोहत है सिरराज रना
जीव ब्रह्म क्षण में हो जावे फिर कैसा होना मरना
अमर होय अमरा पद पावे यह गुण कहिए गुरु वचना
चरणदास गुरु पूरे पाए जग का सुख दुख क्यों सहना
सहजो बाई व्याधि मिटी सब आनन्द मंगल में रहना॥१॥

PART 7: RAGAS ON THE WORD

1 *Gauri Raga*

Bowing low, I take shelter in you

When I meditate on you,
        my doubts and fears disappear,
        my mind and senses are subdued.
Sorrow and poverty cease.
        By your grace,
        the heavy bonds of karma fall away.
This world and the next are set aright.
When I touch your feet,
        my inclinations are transformed,
the way the touchstone turns base metals to gold,
the way raindrops turn to pearls when the moon is full,
        fit for the crown of a king.
The soul becomes Brahma in an instant.
        How can there be any more death?
On gaining immortality, one becomes a god.
        Such is the effect of the Guru's words.
I have found Charandas, the Perfect Master.
Why should I bother with the joy and sorrow of the world?
Sahajo Bai's afflictions have been erased.
        I have been blessed by him.
        I am truly happy.

2 ॥राग सोरठ॥

हमारे गुरु बचन की टेक,

आन धर्मन नाहिं जानू जपूं हरि हरि एक
गुरु बिना को पार तारे धरो नाना भेष
करो तीरथ वरत राखो होहु पंडित शेख
गुरु विना नहि ज्ञान दीपक हरे घट अंधियार
काम क्रोध रु लोभ मांहि पागिया संसार
कर दया रण जीत श्री गुरु दियो मंतर कान
"सहज" घट प्रकाश हुआ मिटो सब अज्ञान॥२॥

3 ॥राग मल्हार॥

हमारे गुरु पूरण दातार

अभय दान दीन न को दीने कीने भव जल पार
जनम जनम के बंध काटे यम बंधन दिए जार
रंक हुते सो राजा कीने हरि धन दियो अपार
देवे ज्ञान भक्ति पुनि देवें योग बतावन हार
तनमन वचन सकल सुखदाई हिरदय बुधि उजियार
सब दुख गंजन पातक भंजन करुणा सिंधु अपार
सज्जन दुर्जन जो चलि आवे एकहि दृष्टि निहार
आनन्द रूप स्वरूप मई हैं लिप्त नहिं संसार
चरणदास गुरु सहजिया के नमो बारम्बार॥३॥

2 *Raga Sorath*

Resting on the guru's words

I know nothing of other religions.
    I simply chant "Hari ... Hari".
Without the guru,
    who can take me across the ocean of existence,
    no matter what else they claim to be?
Making pilgrimages, fasting,
    even pandits and sheikhs
    never find knowledge.
Without the lamp of the guru
    the body remains in darkness,
One lives in passion, anger and greed,
    and drowns in the world.
In his compassion, Ranjit ji,
    Shri Guru, whispered the mantra to me.
Sahajo's body was filled with light,
    my ignorance vanished.

3 *Raga Malhar*

Our guru gives everything perfectly

He gives courage to the humble,
    and takes them across the ocean of existence.
He cuts the ties of many lives
    and burns Yama's bonds.
He turns a pauper into an emperor,
    by sharing the unspeakable wealth of Hari with them.
He gives knowledge and devotion,
    and teaches true yoga.
His words give happiness to the mind and body,
    they enlighten the heart with wisdom.
He destroys all sorrows, removes all sins,
    he is an unfathomable ocean of compassion.
Whoever comes to him, the good and the bad,
    are equal in his eyes.

4 ॥राग मल्हार॥

ऐसे जन धन जननी जिन जाए

ढूंसर कुलमें भक्ति नहीं थी ताकूं तारन आए
कारण परमारथ तन धारो बहुतक जीव उबारे
केवट हो भवसागर माहीं शरण लगे सो तारे
मुक्ति स्वरूप भूप मन जीते आसा सकल जलाई
भक्ति खेत में लोभ खरथुवा ताकूं दिया मिटाई
ज्ञान योग के सूरज प्रगटे वाणी किरन पसारी
चार दिशा में भया उजाला चौंक उठे नर नारी
प्रेम झलाझल नैनन माहीं हिरदय शीतल ताई
नख, शिख, शील, संतोष क्षमा है बरनै सहजोबाई॥४॥

He is the embodiment of bliss, god's true form,
    he is not sullied by the world.
Charandas is Sahajiya's guru,
    I bow before him, again and again.

4 *Raga Malhar*

Blessed is the one to whom mother gave birth

There was no devotion in the Dhusar line,
    you came to be their saviour.
For the sake of the Supreme Soul,
    you assumed a human body
    and rescued many people.
You are a boatman
    in the ocean of existence.
    Whoever takes refuge in you
    will be saved.
You are the embodiment of liberation,
    you conquer the minds of kings,
    you calm our fears.
The wild weeds of greed grew in the garden of devotion,
    you destroyed them all.
You are the sun of knowledge and yoga,
    your words are filled with their light.
Their brightness shines in the four directions,
    dazzling men and women.
You fill their eyes with endless love
    and comfort their hearts.
From head to toe
    you are virtue, peace and forgiveness,
    says Sahajo Bai.

5 ॥राग मल्हार॥

सखि री धन धरनी धन देशा

धन "डैहरा" मेवात मध्य जो हरी आए जन भेषा
धन भादों धन तीज सुदी है धन दिन मंगल कारी
धन द्रूसर कुल बालक जनम्यो मुदित भएनर नारी
धन धन माई कुंजो रानी धन मुरलीधर ताता
अगले दत्तव अब फलपायो तिनके सुत भए ज्ञाता
भर्म नसावन भक्ति बढ़ावन बहु पारायण करता
सब फल दायक सब कुछ लायक अघमौचनदुखहर्ता
अनगिन वर्ष बहुत चिर जीवो गुरु शुकदेब सहाई
सहजो बाई देत असीसें पावै दरश बधाई ॥५॥

6 ॥राग मल्हार॥

सखि आज जन्मे लीला धारी,

तिमिर भजैगो भक्ति बढ़ेगी पारायण नर नारी।
दरशन करते आनन्द उपजे नाम लिए अघनाशे,
चरचा में संदेह मिटेसब खुले हियेकी गांसे।
बहुतक जीव किए भवपारा आवा गवन न होई,
यम के दंड दहन पावक की, तिनकूँ मूल निकोई।
हुइ है प्रेमी योगी ज्ञानी ब्रह्म रूप हो जाई,
चरणदास पर मारथ कारण प्रगटे सहजो बाई॥६॥

5 *Raga Malhar*

Dear friend, blessed is the earth, blessed the land

Blessed is Dahara in the land of Mevat,
    where Hari came, disguised as a man.
Blessed is the month of Bhadon,
    blessed was that auspicious Tuesday.
Blessed is the Dhusar lineage
    into which the child was born,
    all were happy when they saw him.
Blessed indeed is mother Kunjo Rani,
    blessed his father Muralidhar.
They must have given great gifts in a previous life
    to receive such a reward:
    their son became a scholar.
By reading the scriptures
    he destroys doubt and spreads devotion.
He bears much fruit and can do many things.
    He removes sin and smashes sorrow.
May he live forever, through countless ages,
    guru Shukdev be our helper.
He blesses Sahajo Bai each time she beholds him,
    I am fortunate indeed.

6 *Raga Malhar*

Dear friend, Krishna is born today

On hearing him read the scriptures,
    darkness vanishes and devotion grows.
On seeing him, bliss is born.
On taking his name, one becomes indestructible.
On talking with him, doubts are erased,
    and the knots of the heart are released.
He carries many beings across the ocean of existence
    and they are never reborn again.
Yama's clubs are burnt like sticks in a fire,
    they are like straw torn from the ground.
He can make you a lover, a yogi, a sage.
Charandas was born to reveal the highest truth,
    says Sahajo.

7 ॥राग मल्हार॥

सखिरी जन्म लियो सुखदाई।

ढूंसर कुल में परगट हुए बजत अनन्द बधाई,
भादो तीज सुदी दिन मंगल सात घडीदिन आये।
सत्रह से अरु साठ हुतो तब संवत जब प्रगटाए
जै जैकार हुओ नभ मांही मात पिता मुखदेखो।
जानत हुइ है कौन पुरुष यह आयो है नर भेखो,
जगत चलावन अगम पंथको सूरज भक्ति उदयको
आप गुपाल साधु तन धारो निश्चय मोमन ऐसो
गुरु शुकदेव नाम धर दीनो चरणदास उपकारी।
सहजो बाई तन मन वारे बारबार बलिहारी॥७॥

8 ॥राग मल्हार॥
सखि री आज आनन्द देत बधाई,

सत गुरु ने अवतार लियो है हिल मिलमंगल गाई
अद्भुत लीला कहा बखानूं मोपै कही न जाई,
बहु विधि बाजे बाजनलागे सुनतहियो हुलसाई
धन भादों धन तीज सुदी है जादिन प्रगटे आई,
धन धन कुंजो भाग्य तिहारो चरणदास सुत पाई
कल्युग में हरि भक्तिचलाकर जनकी करीसहाई,
श्रीशुक देव करीजब किरपा गावे सहजो बाई॥८॥

7 Raga Malhar

Dear friend, he who gives happiness is born

When he manifested himself in the Dhusar lineage,
joyful shouts rang out.
It was the month of Bhadon, the third day of the lunar fortnight,
the light half of the month, Tuesday,
early in the morning,
1760 on the Vikram calendar[1], when he was born.
Cries of "*Jaya!*" "*Jaya*!" filled the sky,
when his parents saw his face;
they knew which soul had come in the form of a man.
The sun of devotion rose
to return the world to the path of true religion.
He is Gopal, dressed in the body of a sadhu,
I am certain of this.
The benevolent guru Shukdev called him "Charandas".
Again and again, I offer my body and mind to him.
Sahajo Bai is devoted to her guru.

8 Raga Malhar

Dear friend, today bliss rejoices

The true guru has become incarnate,
let us praise the avatar.
How can I describe this wonderful game?
I know I cannot.
Let the musical instruments play,
that we may hear them and rejoice.
Blessed is the month of Bhadon,
blessed be the third day of the lunar fortnight,
the day of his birth.
Blessed, blessed is Kunjo,
you are fortunate to have Charandas as your son.
He established Hari-bhakti in Kaliyuga,
to help us,
thanks to the mercy of Shri Shukdev
says Sahajo Bai.

---

1 1703 A.D.

9 ॥राग बिलावल॥

मुकट लटक अटकी मन माहीं,
नृतत नट वर मदन मनोहर।
कुँडल झलक अलक बिथराई,
नाक बुलाक हलत मुक्ताहल।
होठ मटक गति भौंह चलाई,
छुमुकं ढुमुक पग धरत धरनि पर।
बांहि उठाय करत चतुराई,
झुनक झुनक नूपुर झन कारत।
ताता थेई ताता थेई रिझत रिझाई,
चरणदास सहजो हिय अंतर।
भवन करो नित शुक मुनि राई॥९॥

10 ॥राग काफी॥

नयनो लख लैनी सांई तेरे हजूर,

आगे पीछे दाहिने वाऐं सकल रहा भर पूर।
जिनको ज्ञान गुरु का नाही सो जानत है दूर,
योग यज्ञ तीरथ ब्रत साधे, पावत नाही कूर।
स्वर्ग मृत्यु पाताल उसी में, सोई हरि का नूर,
चरणदासगुरुमोहि बताये, सहजो सबका मूर॥१०॥

9 *Raga Bilaval*

I remember his long crown,
Natavara dancing,
Madan, the thief of hearts,
his large ear-rings
briefly glimpsed through his curls,
the pearl hanging from his nose,
the movement of his lips
and the rise and fall of his eyebrows,
the quickness of his feet
against the earth,
the skill with which he raised his arms,
the jingle-jangle of his ankle bells,
tata-thei, tata-thei,
he was enchanted
and he enchanted us all.
Charandas lives in Sahajo's heart.
Make me your home, Shuk Muni Rai,
Lord of Delight and Restraint.

10 *Raga Kaphi*

Eyes, behold your lord, the Master

In front of you, behind you, to the right and the left,
He fills the whole universe.
Those who do not know the guru
think that God is far away.
When they fast, contort their bodies,
undertake long pilgrimages
and still cannot find Him,
they decide that God is cruel.
Hari's light fills the heavens,
the earth and the nether regions.
Charandas told me:
He is the source of all there is, Sahajo.

11 ॥राग काफी॥

हरि हरि जप लेना अवसर बीत्यो जाय,

जोदिनगएसोफिर नहि आवें करविचारमन लाय
यह जग बाजी साँच न जानो तामें मत भर माय।
कोई किसी का है नहिं बौरे नाहक लिए लगाय,
अंतसमय कोई काम न आवे जबयमतोहिबुलाय।
चरणदासकहै सहजोबाई सतसंगत सिरनाय॥११॥

12 ॥राग बिलावल॥

हरि बिन तेरो नाहिं हितू कोई या जग मांहि

अंत समय तू देख ले कोई गहे न बांही
यम से कहा छुड़ा सके कोई संगन होई,
नारी हूं छुट गई, रही स्वारथ को रोई,
पुत्र कलतर कौन के भाई अरु बंधा।
सब ही तोहि जलाय है समझे नहिं अन्धा,
महल दृव्य ह्याँई रहै पचि पचि कर जोड़ा
गज बाहन ठाडे रहे चाकर अरु घोड़ा
पर काजैं दुख सुख सहे हरि सुमरण खोया
सहजो बाई यम गहे जब सिर धुन रोया॥१२॥

11 *Raga Kaphi*

Chant "Hari, Hari!"
Time passes quickly,
    and will not come again.
Chant the Name,
    keep it always in your mind.
The universe is a gamble,
    it is not true,
    do not be deceived.
You are no one's,
    no one is yours.
You are mad to cling
    to those you cannot keep.
When Yama calls you
    at the end of your life,
    no one can help you.
Charandas says:
    submit to good company,
    Sahajo Bai.

12 *Raga Bilaval*

Without Hari,
    no one cares for you in this world.
When you die, you will see,
    no one will take you by the arm,
No one can keep Yama away,
    no one will go with you.
When your pulse stops,
    they will weep for themselves.
Your wife and sons, brothers and relatives
    will no longer be yours.
They burn you before you die,
    you are blind and cannot see it.
You worked hard for your palace, your wealth,
    and can take nothing with you.
Your elephants and bearers, servants and horses,
    will be left behind you, lamenting.

13 ॥राग आसावरी॥

बाबा काया नगर बसाओ

ज्ञान दृष्टि से घटमें देखो सुरत निरत मनलाओ
पांच मार मन बसकर अपनो तीनों ताप नसाओ
सत संतोष गहो दृड़ता से दुर्जन मार भगाओ
शील क्षमा धीरज कूं धारो अनहद बंब बजाओ
पाप बानिया रहन न दीजे धर्म बजार लगावो।
सूबस वास होय जब नगरी बैरी रहे न कोई
चरणदासगुरुअमल बतायो सहजो संभले सोई॥१३॥

14 ॥राग सोरठ॥

भयामन हरि रस पी मतवारा रे

आठ पहर झूमत हीबीते डार दिया सब भारा रे
इडा पिंगला ऊपर पहुंचे सुषमन घाट उघाड़ा रे
पीवन लगे सुधा रस जबही दुर्जन भगे विकारा रे
गंग जमन बिच आसन मारा चमकचमकचमकारे
चित स्थिर चंचल मन थाका पांचों का बल हारा
चरणदासकिरपासेसहजोभरमकरमभए छारारे॥१४॥

You were sometimes happy and sometimes sad,
you worked hard, but forgot Hari.
Sahajo Bai says:
When Yama seizes you,
you will weep, you will wail.

13 *Raga Asavari*

Beloved master, live in me

Having the eyes of knowledge,
look into your body.
Unite the embodied soul and the Absolute
in your mind.
Kill the five senses,
control your thoughts,
destroy the cravings
of the spiritual, supernatural and physical worlds.
Hold tightly to contentment and truth.
Avoid the wicked.
Adorn yourself with virtue, forgiveness and patience.
Play the drum of unstruck sound.
Drive out the sinful shopkeepers,
deal with those who are interested in dharma.
When good people live in your city,
you will have no enemies.
My guru, Charandas, told me this trick,
Sahajo relies on him.

14 *Raga Sorath*

My mind was drunk on Hari's nectar

My body swayed the whole day,
I was completely weightless.
The psychic channels of Ida and Pingala
met in the lake of Sushumna.
I drank the nectar of immortality
and my evil inclinations left me.
As I settled at the conjunction
of the Ganges and the Yamuna,
I was dazzled, dazzled, dazzled.

15 ॥राग बसन्त॥

आयौ बसन्त धन मेरे भाग पाँचों गावें एक राग

और पचीसो उ़नके संग सोभी भीगे सरस रँग
मतवारा भयामनजु भूपबिसरगयावह निजस्वरूप
रही न कुछ तन की संभार मगन भयो बार बार
कही न जाय उपज्यो अनन्द औरखेलसबभएमन्द
तिरवेनी तट कर बिहार पीवन बैठा अमी धार
ज्योति बाल पूजे जुदेव अगम अगोचरलहो भेब
शीश भेट दीनोजु जाय दरशन कीने अतिअघाय
चरण दास गुरु दईसेन सहजोबाई भयो चैन॥१५॥

16 ॥राग बसंत॥

आतमः पूजा अधिकीजानसकलशिरोमणियाहीमान

विस्तारो हितभवनमाहिंभरमदृष्टिजहां पड़ेनाहिं
हिरदय कोमलठौरलीप कर विचार जहां धूप धीप
या सेवा का दया मूल समता चन्दन क्षमाफूल
मधुर बचनसोइबालभोग निंदा झूटनतजअयोग
घन्टा अनहद सुरत लाव घटघट देखोएक भाव
करो सुखीसुख आप लेव या पूजासूँ सुखी देव
चरणदास गुरू कहयो मोहिसोहँसोहँ जाप होहि
इन्द्री बुधमन तहँलगावसहजोऐसोनाहिं दाव॥१६॥

My higher mind settled, my lower mind grew weary,
    my senses fell back, defeated.
By the grace of Charandas,
    Sahajo's confusion and past karma
    turned to ash.

15 *Raga Basant*

Spring has come. I am blessed,
    my five senses sing one song,
as do the twenty-five elements
    which are bathed in delight.
My mind was intoxicated.
    The king declared a holiday.
I lost all awareness of my body,
    my consciousness faded away again and again.
How can I describe the bliss I felt?
    All other games were of no account.
Having come to the place where the three rivers meet,
    I sat and drank the nectar stream.
A radiant child was there, resplendent like a god,
    invisible, incomprehensible,
    and I worshipped him.
I bowed and gazed on him for a very long time.
    Guru Charandas raised his hand
    and I was content.

16 *Raga Basant*

The worship of the self is the best,
    there is none greater.
Expand your consciousness within your soul,
    where no distractions lie.
Scrub the inner sanctum of your heart,
    light lamps and incense there.
Such worship is the root of all compassion,
    apply the sandalwood paste of
    even-mindedness,
    offer the flowers of forgiveness.
Let your soft words
    be morning food for the gods.

17 ॥राग बसंत॥

ऐसो बसँत नहि बार बारतैं पाई मनुषा देह सार

यह अवसरविंरथान खोयभक्तिबीजहिय धरन बोय
सत गँगत कोसीच नीरसत गुरूजी सूँकरो सीर
नीकी बाड़ विचारदेव परनराख या कूँ जु सेव
रखवारी कर हेत हेत तबही उपजे प्रेम खेत
खोट कपटपँछी उड़ाय मोह घास नहिं उगनपाय
सँभले बारी नोऊ अँग प्रेम फूल फूले उमँग
पुहुप गूँथ माला बनाव आदिपुरुष कूंजा चढाव
कहेसहजोबाईचरणदासपुरवोमममनकीसकल आस॥१७॥

18 ॥राग बसंत॥

मिलीगावोसाधोयहबसँतहेंअविगतिलीलाअगमपँथ

जहांनाम पदारथ हैइकंग नहिंपइहैदूजा औ़र रंग
जहांदरसैसाधोरामएकनहिपइहैदूजा कोई और भेख
जहांज्ञानध्यानकोलगोतारजहाँ आपविराजेओंकार
सबघटघटव्यापकनिराकारकोईनहिं पावे यहविचार
जहाँ ब्रह्म अखण्डित अति अनूप,
जाहि सुर मुनि योगी जपें भूप
जोछायरहोहैंसर्वमांहि बाबिननहिंखालीकोईठांहि
गुरूचरणदासपूरनऔतारनिजकृपादेयजगव्याधिटार
सहजोबाईनितनायशीशमेरेगुरू मेरे सकलईश॥१८॥

He who does not abandon slander and lies
is no yogi.
Ring the bell of unstruck sound,
fill your body with one simple emotion.
Make others happy. Be happy yourself.
This is the worship which will make the gods happy.
Guru Charandas told me:
chant "Soham, Soham",
with all your senses, mind and intellect,
let it come, Sahajo, of its own accord.

17 *Raga Basant*

Spring passes quickly. A human birth is rare,
do not waste this opportunity.
Sow the seeds of devotion in the soil of your heart.
Water them with the Ganges of good company.
Cultivate an attachment to the true guru.
Fence your garden with good thoughts and discipline.
Chase the birds of deceit away, pull out the weeds.
Prune away attachment so that new thoughts joyfully sprout.
Make a garland of the flowers and offer them to Adipurusha.
Sahajo says:
Charandas pervades my whole mind.

18 *Raga Basant*

It is spring. Sing, good people, of His endless games
on the path to the Inaccessible.
In the presence of the Name,
you need no other devotion.
When the saints see Rama, they see only Rama,
The divine assumes no other shape.
Together knowledge and devotion weave a thread
on which the flowers of Om make an endless garland.
The formless one pervades the body.
He is beyond all that we can think.
Brahma is indivisible. He is most splendid.

19 ॥होरी राग धनाश्री॥

साधो मन माया के रंग जगत सब रंग रह्यो।

मूरख भए खेल में अन्धरे नाना स्वाँग बनाय
आसा धरि धरि नाचन लागे चोवा चाह लगाय
योग करें सिधि आठों चाहे मान बड़ाई हेत
राज वासना भोग लोक के काशी करवत लेत
पच अगनी बहुतापन लागेबहुत अधः मुख झूल
बहुतक दौड़ें अठसठ तीरथ ज्ञान भक्ति गये भूल
चरणदास गुरु तत्व बतायो दीन्हें खेल छुड़ाय
सहजोबाई शीश नवाए बार बार बलिजाय॥१९॥

20 ॥होरी राग धना श्री॥

मैं तो खेलूं प्रभु के संग होली रँग भरी

जित देखूँ तित रमि रह्यो सबमें व्यापक है हरी
सब कुछ भयोदियोसुखजनकूँ अद्भुत लीलाहीकरी
नाना जतनकियेमिलवेके प्रीतम पायो हम घरही
पावत सभी भरम भय भागे जनममरनकीकटीलरी
जीवनमुक्त भयो मन मेरो व्याधा सकल जरी
अमरलोकपदफगुआपायो जनममरणकीविपतटरी
चरणदासगुरुकिरपाकिनी सहजोहियआनन्दभरी॥२०॥

Gods, sages and yogis chant His Name.
He is everything
    and nothing exists outside of Him.
Guru Charandas is a complete incarnation of God.
By your mercy, keep the world's afflictions from us.
Sahajo Bai bows her head to Him each day.
He is my guru, my entire God.

19 *Holi Raga Ghanashri*

Oh saints, the world has many colours,
    the mind sparkles with illusion.
Like fools, we are blind actors in a drama,
    wearing many costumes, always playing the clown.
We hope, and hope, and begin to dance,
    led by the sweet perfume of desire.
Even if you are a great yogi,
    equipped with the eight siddhis,
    what good is your pride and conceit?
Kings who enjoyed the pleasures of this world
    still die under the saw in Kashi.
Some ascetics sit between five fires,
    some hang upside down.
Some run to the sixty-eight pilgrim sites,
    many forget knowledge and devotion.
Charandas, my guru, told me this truth:
    life is a game, don't be attached to it.
Sahajo Bai bows her head again and again
    and sacrifices all she has to him.

20 *Holi Raga Ghanashri*

I play Holi with the Lord,
    scattering bright colours.
Wherever I look, I see Rama.
The world is filled with Hari.
He played wonderful cosmic games
    and made everyone happy.
We searched for the Beloved high and low
    and found Him at home.

21 ॥राग होरी॥

साधो भव सागर काल होरी खेलई

भांति भांति के रोगलिए कर करतजीवकी घात
बूढ़ा बाला कछु नहिं देखे देखे दिन नहिं रात
निश्चय मौत सीस मँडराती नाना रँग सँभार
बड़े बड़े अभिमानी मानी सोभी लीने मार
सूरज चन्द जु भयते कापैं स्वर्ग माहिं सब देव
तन धारी सब ही थर्राने ज्ञानी जाने भेव
आपन की देही नहिं माने जाने आतम सांच
चरणदासकहि सहजोबाईताहि न आवे आंच॥२१॥

When I found Him,
    my doubts and fears vanished,
the cycle of birth and death
    was broken,
my mind was liberated,
    my afflictions were destroyed.
I found eternity
    in the revels of Holi.
By the grace of Charandas, my guru,
Sahajo's heart was filled with bliss.

21 *Raga Holi*

O good people, Death plays Holi too,
    across the realm of existence,
scattering diseases with his hand,
    killing living creatures.
He does not care whether you be young or old,
    he does not care whether it is night or day.
Death hovers above all of us,
    holding many colours,
    destroying even the proud and the haughty.
The sun and the moon tremble before him,
    the gods in heaven too.
Everything that has a body
    is afraid of death.
But the wise know a secret:
    the body is false,
    only the soul is true.
Charandas said:
Sahajo Bai, if you know this,
you will never enter the fire.

22 ॥राग ललित॥

सुमिर सुमिर नरउतरोपार भवसागरकीतीक्षणधार

धर्मजहाजमाहिं चढ लीजे संभलसंभलतामेंपगदीजे
शुभकरमनको संगीकीजेहरि मारग की लगेबयार
वादवान पुनिताहि चलावैपापभरेतो हलनहिं पावे
कामक्रोध लूटन कूँ आवें सावधान होकरो संभार
मान पहाड़ीतहांअरत है आशा तृश्नाभंवरपरत है
पाँचमच्छजहाँ चोटकरतहैज्ञानआँखबचचलोनिहार
ध्यानधनीका हृदय धारे गुरु कृपा से लगे किनारे
जब तेरीवह बाँहिपकर ले जन्ममरण दुखदेवें टार
चौथेपदमेंआनंद पावै याजग में तू बहुरन आवें
चरणदासगुरुदेव बतावैसहजोबाई यहीविचार॥२२॥

22 *Raga Lalit*

O mankind, by chanting the Holy Name,
you can cross the swift currents
of the ocean of existence.
Settle yourself carefully
in dharma's ship.
Take virtuous deeds as your companion.
Let Hari supply the breezes you need.
Good deeds will fill your sails.
Evil deeds will leave them flat.
Passion and anger are pirates,
beware when you see them sail near.
The whirlpools of desire hide
behind the peaks of vanity.
When five sharks attack your boat,
the wise sailor can help you get clear.
Let meditation on the Master be your guide.
By the guru's mercy, you can reach the other shore;
when he holds your arm,
you will be saved from the sorrows
of birth and death.
The fourth stage is filled with bliss:
you will never be born again.
Guru-deva Charandas said:
Sahajo Bai, remember this.

23 ॥राग ललित॥

जागिजागि जो सुरमण करै आपतरैऔरनले तरै

हरिकीभक्तिमाँहिचितदेवेपद पंकजबिन औरन सेवै
आनधर्मकूं संगन लेवै फलन कामना सबपरिहरै
काल ज्वालसबहीछुटजावै जनममरनकीठौरनसावै
यौनीसंकट फिर नहीं आवै बार बार जन्मै नहिमरै
ऊँचीपदवी जगमें पावै राजा राणा शीश नवावैं
तनछूटे जा मुक्ति समावै जोपै ध्यान धनी का धरै
ह्याँ के सुख जो जानेकूराचरण कमलमेंलागेपूरा
वेग संभारेसोजनसूराचरणदाससहजोहो अरै॥२३॥

24 ॥राम रमन॥

ज्यों त्यों राम नाम ही तारै॥ टेक

जान अजान अग्नि ज्यों छूवै वह जारै पै जारै
उलटा सुलटा बीच गिरै ज्यों धरती मांहि जैसे
उपजि रहै निश्चय करि जानो हरि सुमरण है तैसे
वेद पुराण मैं मथ काढ़ा राम नाम तत सारा
तीन लोकमें सकल शिरोमणि पापजलावन हारा
हृदय शुद्ध करे मन निर्मल ऊँची पदवी देवै
चरणदासकहै सहजोबाई व्याधासब हर लेवै॥२४॥

23 Raga Lalit

He who is awakened,
        and always chants the Name of the Lord,
crosses the ocean of existence
        and takes others with him.
Give your mind in devotion to Hari.
        Do not serve the lotus-feet of other teachers.
Do not follow other religions.
        Abandon the desire for reward.
You will be released from the flames of death.
        You will escape the cavern of birth and death.
You will never endure the perils of birth,
        You will never be born, you will never die.
The True Master holds high status in the world,
        even kings and emperors bow before him.
Let go of the body and you will be liberated,
        when you meditate on the Master.
Whoever knows the world to be trash
        will cling to the lotus-feet of the true Master.
The needs of the brave are quickly granted.
Charandas said:
        Sahajo, be courageous.

24 Raga Raman

I do not know why, but only the name of Ram can save me (chorus)

Touch the fire deliberately, touch it by accident,
        it will still burn you, it will burn.
Plant the seed up, plant the seed down,
        it will still grow, it will grow.
Hari's Name is like that.
        It is the essence of the Vedas and Puranas.
        It is supreme in the three worlds.
        It destroys sins, purifies the heart,
        cleanses the mind, it can make you mighty.
Charandas said:
        Sahajo, it will carry away all your afflictions.

25 ॥राग रामकली॥

अब तुम अपनी ओर निहारी॥ टेक

हमारे अवगुणपरमतजाओतुमही अपनोविरदसंभारो
युग युग साख तुम्हारी ऐसी वेद पुरान गाई
पतितउधारण नामतुम्हारो यहसुनकैमनदृढ़ता आई
मैं अजान तुम सब कुछ जानो घटघट अन्तर्यामी
मैं तो चरण तुम्हारे लागी होकृपालु, दयालुजु स्वामी
हाथ जोर मैं अरजकरत हूं अपनाओ गई बांही
द्वार तिहारे आय गिरी मैं पौरुष गुण कुछ नांही
चरणहि दाससहजिया तेरी दर्शनकी निधि पाऊँ
लगनलगी अरुप्राण अड़े हैं तुम को छोड़औरकितजाऊँ॥२५॥

26 ॥राग भैरव॥

हमबालकतुममात हमारीपलपलमाहिकरो रखवारी

निसिदिनगोदीही मेंराखो इतउतचित्त नलावनभाषो
विषय ओरजानेनहिं देओ दुरदुरजाउं तोगहि लेओ
मैंअनजानकछुनहींजानूँ बुरीभलीकूं ना पहिचानूँ
जैसी तैसीतुम हीचीनौगुरुहोध्यानखिलौना दीनो
तुमरी रक्षाही सूँ जीऊं नाम तुम्हारो अमृत पीऊँ
दृष्टि तुम्हारी ऊपर मेरे सदा रहूं मैं शरणें तेरे
मारोझिड़को तोनहिंजाऊँ सरकसरकतुमहीपैआऊँ
चरणदासकीसहजोदासीहोरक्षकपूरण अविनासी॥२६॥

25 *Raga Ramakali*

Look into your heart (chorus)

Do not consider our sins,
 remain in your glory.
For endless ages,
 the Vedas and Puranas have sung of your majesty.
Your name saves the fallen,
 on hearing it, the mind is strengthened.
I am ignorant, you know everything,
 you live in us all.
I cling to your feet,
 be merciful, be kind, dear master.
With hands folded, I make this request:
 make me your own, take my arm.
I wait at your door,
 a woman without any greatness.
A servant at your feet,
 Sahajiya pleads for the gift of a glance.
I reverence you and offer my life to you.
 If I left you, where could I go?

26 *Raga Bhairava*

We are your children, you are our mother,
 look after us each moment.
Hold us in your lap, day and night,
 do not let our minds crawl here and there.
Do not allow me to fall into sensuality,
 if I go astray, restrain me quickly.
I am ignorant, knowing nothing.
 I cannot tell what is good, what is bad.
But despite my foolishness, you do know.
 You are my guru.
 You gave me the toy of meditation.
My life is protected by you.
 I drink the nectar of your name,
 and I am immortal.
Watch over me always
 and I will always have your shelter.

27 ॥राग सोरठ॥

जग में कहा कियो तुम आय,

स्वान की ज्यों पेट भरके दियो जनम गंवाय
पहर पिछले नाहिं जागो कियो ना शुभ कर्म
आन मारग जाय लाग्यो लियो ना गुरु धर्म
जप न कीयो, तपन साध्यो दियो ना तें दान
बहुत उरझयो मोह मदमें कियो काया मान
देह घर है मौत का रे आन काढ़े तोहि
एक क्षण नहिं रह न पावे फिर किए का होहि
रैन दिन आरा बना काटै जु तेरी आय।
सत गुरु कहै सुन सहजिया अबकरो भजनउपाय॥२७॥

Even if you beat me and scold me,
I will never leave you,
each time I will come crawling back again.
Sahajo is Charandas' servant,
he is my protector, complete in every way,
he is indestructible.

27 *Raga Sorath*

Why did you come into this world?

If you live like a dog
merely filling your stomach,
your life will be wasted.
If you do not wake up before dawn,
if you do not act virtuously,
if you follow another path,
if you disregard the guru's teachings,
if you do not chant God's name,
if you practise no austerities,
if you do not share your wealth,
you will be entangled in illusion,
drunkenness and the pride of the flesh.
The body is the home of death,
death will come and take you away.
You cannot live a moment longer.
What use will your body be to you then?
Night and day are like a saw,
cutting away at the span of your life.
The sat-guru said:
Sahajiya, salvation comes
when you praise the Lord's Name.

28 ॥राग कान्हरा॥

सठ तज राम जगत सूं राच्यो

जिहिं कारन बहु स्वांग भरेसें चौरासी में नाच्यो
गरभमाहिंजोबचनकियेथे एक हुबारभयोनहिसांच्यों
स्वारथही कूं उठउठ धायोरामभगत परमारथत्यागों
संतनकीटकसालचढ़ोनहिंगुरुकीहटकभूंनाजाँच्यों
पंचविषयकेमदमेंमातोअभिमानीहोयबहुतकमाचो
यमद्वारेकाभयनहितोकूँ नरकअग्निमेंजहैताचो
चरणदासकहैसहजोबाईहरिकीशरणगहैसोईसाँचो ॥२८॥

29 ॥राग सारंग॥

हमारे औषधि नाम धनी का

आधि व्याधि तनमनकी खोवे शुद्धकरेवह नीका
अमरभएजिनजिनयह खाईभव नगरीनहिं आवे
दृढ़ मतिहोय पथ्य वही राखे सत गुरु वैद्य बतावे
संत संगत का भवन बना करपरदालाज लगावै
जगत वासनापवनचलतअतिसो लगने नहिपावें
शुभ कर्म नलै टेक टहलुआ दीपक ज्ञानजलावै
नित्यअनित्य विचारसार गहिदूरअसार बगावे
जीव रूप यों रोग भगै जब ब्रह्म रूप हो जावे
सहजोबाई सुनंहुलसावे चरणदास बतलावे॥२९॥

28 *Raga Kanhara*

Wicked man, having abandoned Ram, you created the world

Therefore you played the fool
and danced your way through eighty-four lakh births.
The promises that you made in the womb
never came true, not even once.
Driven by selfishness, you ran and ran,
heedless of the highest truth,
devotion to Ram.
You were not assayed in the mint of the saints,
you were never tested in the guru's shop
Intoxicated by the objects of the senses,
you were excited by your own vanity.
Yama is at your door,
have you no fear?
You fool, you will burn in the fires of hell.
Charandas said:
Sahajo Bai, whoever takes refuge in Hari
is a true and honest person

29 *Raga Sarang*

The name of the Guru is the best medicine

He can cure the troubled mind and the ailing body
– better than anyone else.
If you take the medicine he prescribes
you will live forever and never be born again.
Doctor Sat Guru prescribes a wholesome diet,
which can strengthen the will.
He recommends time in the company of the holy
and protects his patients with modest surroundings,
in a world where the winds of passions rage,
and modesty is decidedly unfashionable.

30 ॥राग सारंग॥

तेरी लीला अधिक सुहावनि

देख देख कर मन हुलसति है संतनके मनभावनि
सतगुणरचिब्रह्मण्ड बनायोअधरधरो है अ रजयही
भाँति भांतिके रंगरँग रहयो सातद्वीप नौ खँडही
स्वर्गमृत्यु पाताल रचे सब इच्छा सों त ्कालही
माया अगम अपार तिहारी बरणसकेनहींवेद ही
तीन गुणनतक बुधपहुचत है परै तुम्हारो भेदही
क्षणमेंउत्पत्ति क्षणमें परलयजो चाहो सबकछुबनै
चरणदासगुरु दृष्टिदईजबगुणवाद सहजोभनै॥३०॥

With the support of good deeds,
        he trims the lamp of knowledge
and teaches his patients to distinguish
        between the mortal and the immortal,
        to purge away the things that are dangerous to them.
When the disease has been cured,
        the patient becomes the embodiment of Brahma.
Sahajo Bai is happy,
        when Charandas talks like this.

30 *Raga Sarang*

The play was charming

While watching it, the saints were happy,
        it appealed to their hearts and minds.
You created good qualities, the universe,
        and suspended the world in mid-air.
        We were amazed!
In an instant, using all sorts of colours,
        you created the seven continents, the nine regions,
        heaven, the mortal and nether realms.
        You made a wish and they came into being.
Your Maya is inaccessible, unfathomable,
        even the Vedas can not describe it.
The three gunas reach as far as the intellect,
        beyond that is the mystery you do not reveal.
The world is created in an instant,
        the world is destroyed in an instant,
        whatever you want, happens at once.
Guru Charandas knows what lies beyond the gunas.
        Sahajo worships him.

31 ॥राग सारंग॥
परो मन हिय गुण गावन बान

बिन गोपाल और जो भाषे तोहि गुरु की आन
वेद माहिं ब्रह्मा हूं गायो शँकर सींगी माहिं
शेष सहस मुख निस दिन गावे तोहूं पाहि
बीणाले नारद पुनि गावें गायो व्यास उचार
गणपति शारदगान करत नित्त तऊन पायो पार
गुणावाद गावन प्रभु परसन बढे भक्ति कोभाव
गायोसुक मुनिचरणहिदासा सहजोकोहूंचाव ॥३१॥

32 ॥राग पूरवी॥

हरि को कोई न जानत भेद,

शिव ब्रह्मादिकखोजत था के नेति नेति कहेवेद
नाल माहिं ब्रह्मा नहिं आयो, थाकि फिरत केहि कीन
योग ध्यान कर शँकर हारे थाह लेनभए लीन,
भेद न पायो शेष शारदा सुरपति और गणेश
कामदेव, नारद सनकादिक धरे भक्ति का भेष
ज्ञानी, गुणी रिषीमुनि जैते योगेश्वर सिध साध
चरणदास कहे सहजोबाई पँडितपोथी लाद ॥३२॥

31 *Raga Sarang*

My heart endlessly sings His praises

Guru's curse be upon you,
if you speak of anyone but Gopal!
Brahma sings of Him in the Vedas,
Shankar trumpets His glory.
Shesha has a thousand mouths
to worship Him night and day.
Narada honours Him with his veena,
Vyasa proclaims His Name.
Ganapati and Saraswati
sing of Him each day
and still do not exhaust His depths.
With ever-increasing devotion,
wise men sing of the Lord
and are happy.
Shuka Muni and Charandas sing about Hari,
Sahajo would like to, as well.

32 *Raga Purvi*

No one understands the mystery of Hari

Shiva, Brahma, and all the gods,
tried to solve the riddle —
He is "not that", "not this",
say the Vedas.
Brahma came again as a child,
and exhausted himself in asceticism.
Shiva practised Yoga and meditated intently,
without success.
Shesha, Saraswati, Indra and Ganapati
worshipped Him,
without understanding who He is.
Kamadeva, Narada, Sanaka and the other sons of Brahma,
adorned themselves with devotion.

33 ॥राग पूरवी॥

मन तोहि कब उपजे गी सयान

इंद्रिन के रस सों छुटि मूरख पार ब्रह्म गलतान
जगसो पीठकहोकबि दैहो सनमुख हरिकी ओर
साधों की संगतिकब करि हो जगसे नाता तोर
जप करनेकोकबतुम लगिहो चरणकमलकेध्यान
निसदिन आयुघटै तन छीजै मनुषजनमकीहान
तुमजुकहोमैं कालकरूँगो काल काल केहाथ
जा कारण ऐसी मति उपजै सो झूठो है साथ
चरण दास गुरु मोहि बतायो, सहजो हिरदय राख
भजन हि सारबतायो गुरुनेवेद पुराणन भाष॥३३॥

34 ॥राग बिलावल॥
गोविन्द के गुण क्यों नहिं गावो

ममतानींदकहामनसूतो जागिजागिहरिसूंचितलाओ
गुण गावत बहुपतित उबारे ऊँची पदवी दीनी
जातिवरण से ऊंचे कीने आधि व्याधिहरलीनी
भव जल पार भए थिर हुए आवा गमननसायो
वैसी हीतुमरी गति हुई है हरि भज अवसरपायो
अर्ध रात्रिअरु तरुण अवस्थाउठकर ध्यानलगावै
ताकीस्तुतिशेष करत हैशिवब्रह्मादिकसीस नवावें
चरण हि दास बनो पद सेवौ गुरु उपदेश संभारो
सहजोनौधाभक्तिकरीजेआपतिरोऔरनकोतारो॥३४॥

The wise, the moral, rishis and munis,
        Shiva, sidhas and sadhus,
said Charandas,
        the pandits bearing their books
are like donkeys, Sahajo Bai.

33 *Raga Purvi*

When will your mind be mature?

When will you turn from the pleasure of the senses
        and immerse yourself in Parabrahma,
When will you turn your back on the world
        and fix your eyes on Hari?
When will you keep company with the saints
        and break your ties with worldly people?
When will you chant the Name of the Lord
        and meditate on the lotus-feet of the Master?
By day and night, your life grows less,
        the body decays, you have wasted this birth.
Why do you say: "I'll do it tomorrow, tomorrow"?
        Tomorrow you may be dead.
Whoever teaches you this, is a fool.
My guru, Charandas, told me:
        Always remember, Sahajo,
        to sing of the glory of God.
        This is the essence, Charandas said,
of the Vedas, Puranas and all the commentaries.

34 *Raga Bilaval*

Why not sing the virtues of Govinda?

Oh mind, why do you sleep?
        Renounce your attachments, wake up.
        Wake up and remember Hari.
The fallen are saved by singing His virtues,
        they will attain a high position,
        be elevated in caste and status,
        lose their distress and afflictions.

35 ॥राग जै जैवंती॥

दसौ दिशा में देखा तो कूं और कोई नहिं सांई

नखसिखव्यापरहयोसबजगमेंज्योंतागासबमनकोमाही
सिंधुमद्धज्यों लहरेजानो तामेंसब पानी पहचानो
ऐसे नाहीं दूजा ठानो सब जग सांई सांई
परमेश्वर को रूप सकल जग पूर रह्यो सब ठाई,
नाना रूप धार तू प्रगट्यो तेरी गति नहि पाई।
चरणदासगुरुके चरणोंपरबारबार सहजो बलिजाई॥३५॥

36 ॥राग जै जैवंती॥

मेरे एक श्री गोपाल, और नाहिं कोई।

आय बसेहिये माहिं और दूजो कोई ध्यान नाहिं॥
मेरा सब उनके ताहिं, वोई वोई वोई।
जाति हूं कीकान तजी, लोकहू कि लाज भजी
दोनों कुल माहिं सजी, कहा कौ कोई।
उपजी घट प्रीत मेरी, निहचै हुई हूं चेरी॥
पहरि हिये प्रेम बेरी, टुटे नहिं जोई।
मैं तो चरणदास भई, गतिमति सब त्याग दई॥
सहजो अब नाहिं रही, उठ गई है दोई॥ ३६॥

Strengthened, they will cross the ocean of existence,
they will never be born again,
they will never die.
Rise up at midnight, rise again at dawn
and meditate on Hari.
Shesha sings his praises,
Shiva, Brahma and all the gods bow before him.
Charandas is my guru, I obey his commands.
The nine forms of devotion saved me,
they can save you too.

35 *Raga Jaya Jaya Vanti*

I see you in all ten directions,
no one else but you, my master.
You are here, in all the world,
like a thread in a set of beads.
You are like the waves of the sea,
each wave contains the whole ocean.
There is none like you in all the world,
You are my Master, my Master.
The complete embodiment of Parameshwar
in all the world, in every place.
You manifest in many forms
and there is no end to your variety.
Sahajo sacrifices herself
at Charandas' feet,
again and again.

36 *Raga Jaya Jaya Vanti*

I have only Shri Gopal,
I see no one else.
He lives in my heart,
I care for no other.
Everything I have is his,
is his, is his, is his.
I have abandoned the modesty of my caste.
I am not worried what others may think.
I was a bride, between two families,
and no one could stop me.

37 ॥राग परज॥

तेरी गति किन्हु न जानी हो,

ब्रह्मा शेष, महेश्वर थाके बहुतक बखानी हो
चार वेद स्तुति कर थाके चारों वाणी हो
बाद करत सब मतहूं थाके थाके ज्ञानी हो
पाँच तत्व निर्गुण हूं थाके बुद्धि थकानी हो
विद्या पढ़ पढ़ पंडित थाके अरु ब्रह्म ज्ञानी हो
सब के परे जो अनभै हारी थाह न पानी हो
छान बीन कर बहुतक थाके हुई खिसानी हो,
सुर नरमुनिजन गणपति थाके बड़े विज्ञानी हो
चरणदास थकि सहजो बाई भई सिरानी हो॥३७॥

Love lives in my body,
    I am his disciple.
The bonds of love protect me,
    they will never break.
I am become Charandas,
    I have no thoughts or actions of my own.
Sahajo no longer exists.
    The two are one,
    there is no duality.

37 *Raga Paraj*

No one understands the games you play

Brahma, Shesha and Maheshwar grew weary
    talking about you.
The four Vedas grew weary
    singing your praises.
The various sects grew weary
    arguing about you.
The scholars grew weary
    discussing you.
The five elements and God-without-Form grew weary
    trying to understand you.
The pandits grew weary
    learning about you.
The intellectuals grew weary too.
The peace which is beyond all understanding
    grew weary trying to plumb your depths.
Many have investigated Hari, and grown weary,
    because the task was beyond them:
gods, men and women, sages, even Ganapati
    grew weary, despite their wisdom.
Charandas said: exhaust yourself first,
    Sahajo Bai, then rest content.

38 ॥राग परज॥

तेरी गति सब में जानी हो

विधि निषेद करि देखा तो कूं लिया पिछानी हो
दृष्टि अदृष्टि आस सब तेरी वेद बखानी हो
वार वार मध तू ही तू है यह नहिं छानी हो
पांच तत्व निरगुण है तू ही और न आनी हो
तत्पद, त्वंप द असिपद तूही यह न लुकानी हो
तो बिन दूजा नैक न क्यों हूं यह मन आनी हो
चरण दास नहिं सहजो बाई दुई नसानी हो॥३८॥

38 *Raga Paraj*

We know that you live in everything

Having been forbidden to explore your depths,
    Brahma finally saw you and knew.
Sometimes seeing you, sometimes not
    filled with faith, the Vedas praise you.
This side, that side, in the middle,
    is you, only you, this is no secret.
The five elements and the God-beyond-form
    is you, only you, there is none other.
Here, there, in every breath we take,
    is you, only you, this is no secret.
There is none other but you, nothing at all,
    this is my firm conviction.
There is no Sahajo Bai, there is no Charandas,
    there is no duality.

39 ॥राग कड़खा॥

करी मैं दासि जो आपनी जानि कै,
राखि यो दृष्टि तुम सदा नीकी।
और कोई आसरा धरू ना जगत में,
मानियो साँच मैं कहूं ठीकी।
तुही है मात अरु पिता बन्धु तूही,
तु ही कुल नात है गोत मेरा।
तु ही धन धाम, और जीब इस देह का,
तो बिना और दूजा न हेरा।
जाप तेरा करूँ ध्यान हिरदय धरूँ,
समझ कर ज्ञान तोकूँ पिछानूँ।
शरन तेरी गई टेक ऐसी लई
ता बिना आन कूँ नाहिं जानू।
गही जँब शरण विख्यात जग मैं भई,
सकल लज्जा तुम्हीं हो गुसांईं।
कलू के काल में महा भय मान हूं,
निज चरण कमल की राख छाँईं।
कहै सहजो सोऊ हाथ जोडै दोऊ,
शीस नीचा किए दीन धारे।
"राम" चरण दास जी, अरज सुन लीजिए,
तुही है इष्ट आसा हमारे॥३९॥

39 *Raga Karhkha*

If you know me to be yours,
accept me as your servant.
Watch over me always.
I have no other shelter in this world.
This is true. I say it sincerely.
You are my mother, my father,
all my relatives.
You are my lineage,
my kinsfolk and clan.
You are my wealth, my home,
the soul in my body.
I see no one but you.
I praise your name
and meditate on you in my heart.
You are the one
who fulfils all that I know.
I took shelter in you.
I took shelter in you.
I have no one but you.
When I took refuge in you,
the whole world talked about me.
You are my shame, goswami,
you are my honour.
The great fear I feel
in the Kaliyuga
drives me to the shelter of your lotus-feet.
Sahajo says:
I join my hands,
and bow before you, in great humility.
Ram Charandas ji, hear this request.
You are my Lord,
you are my hope.

